BIG DECISIONS FOR SMALL BUSINESS

What You Should Know
Before You Buy a Computer

A Hands On! Computer Book

BIG DECISIONS FOR SMALL BUSINESS

What You Should Know Before You Buy a Computer

LINDA STROSBERG

Data Processing Decisions

HARPER & ROW PUBLISHERS, New York
Cambridge, Hagerstown, Philadelphia, San Francisco,
London, Mexico City, São Paula, Sydney

The names of all computer programs and computers included herein are registered trademarks of their makers.

Sponsoring Editor: John Willig
Project Editor: Mary E. Kennedy
Designer: C. Linda Dingler
Production: Delia Tedoff
Compositor: Haddon Craftsman
Art by: Kim Llewellyn

Cover design by: Steve Sullivan

Library of Congress Cataloging in Publication Data

   Strosberg, Linda
      Big Decisions for Small Business
1. Microcomputers—Purchasing.   2. Small Business—
      Data processing.   I. Title.
HF5548.2.583373   1984   001.64   83-18478
ISBN 0-06-046485-2

Contents

Introduction

"We are living in the computer age." This statement certainly does not come as a surprise to anyone. Unfortunately, there is a generation that grew up before the computer age began, and so there are many people in a state ranging from mild confusion to borderline panic when it comes to computers. The purpose of this book is to reduce the confusion and to dispel the panic. It is addressed to both men and women. The use of "he" in the text implies "she" also.

The example of the automobile will illustrate the book's approach. Most automobiles are conceptually alike. You can read up on the subject, or you can take a course to familiarize yourself with the technical information about the subject. You might explore such things as the way the internal combustion engine works or how the transmission system is built. This doesn't mean that you are going to design and build a car or even that you are going to do the repairs and maintenance on one. You will have a better idea of what the mechanic is talking about or how important the new features are, however, if you know something about the fundamentals. When you are buying, you will be able to evaluate power, performance, and price more intelligently.

This same approach applies to computers. Like automobiles, most computers are conceptually alike. Once you understand the theoretical concepts behind them, you have a basis for evaluating what you read and hear about them. This book will help you to get past the "jargon" into the realm of understanding. At that point you should have realistic expectations about what computers can do. When it comes to buying, you will be better prepared to make that big decision for your small business.

This book is designed for two specific audiences: the general reader, in particular, the small business person, who wishes to inform himself about computers, and the student who is taking an entry-level business computer course. General computer theory is presented with an emphasis on microcomputers.

This is not a "how-to-buy-a-computer" book. There are a sufficient number of books of that kind available to the reader. They do not address the technical and theoretical subjects in the depth presented here. Rather, the information presented in this book encompasses what the reader might wish to know before buying a computer or at the time that he or she becomes curious about "how the thing actually works."

This book is an attempt to present complicated information in simple terms. There is a certain degree of generalization so that the theory can be understood at the layman's level. Purists may be unhappy about certain omissions, but the purpose is to familiarize the reader with concepts.

The topics covered here are the result of an attempt to bring together in one place information that is usually found in many separate sources at much more technical levels.

The book is organized into six chapters. Chapters 2, 3, and 4 deal with information about what the computer processes (data) and about how it works (hardware and software). The first and last two chapters discuss the human side of things. The chapters are:

1. UNDERSTANDING NEEDS (the process of determining system requirements)
2. DATA (the information the business runs on)
3. HARDWARE (the physical components of the computer)
4. SOFTWARE (the logic that runs the computer)
5. IMPACT OF AUTOMATION (the changes a computer causes)
6. THE SEARCH AND THE SOLUTION (a case study)

There is no attempt to discuss specific brands of computers or prices. There are two reasons for this. The first one is that the technology and the offerings of the various manufacturers are changing so rapidly that information of this type becomes out of date too quickly to be useful in a book of this kind. The best sources for specifics are newspapers, periodicals, and trade publications. The second and more important reason is that every situation is unique. It must be evaluated according to its own needs. Often this evaluation should be done with the help of a knowledgeable computer professional.

This book does supply the reader with a comprehensive view of computers. It is designed to be an aid in the decision-making process. The expectation is that once the reader has finished the book, he will realize that the subject of computers is not incomprehensible, and therefore, not to be feared.

BIG DECISIONS FOR SMALL BUSINESS

What You Should Know
Before You Buy a Computer

1

Understanding
Needs

Later on our discussion will concern itself with information about what computers are and how they work. We will study computer literacy and discover the binary nature of a computer and the logical translations that have enabled us to elevate our interactions from the level of the machine to the "humanized" use of software. But first, we are now going to look at our needs for information and the ways that we structure these needs to determine what type of computer system will meet them. Some technical terms are required in this chapter that may be unfamiliar to you. They are explained in the chapters that follow. The index will show you where they are, however, if you want clarification immediately.

RECOGNIZING TROUBLE

Most business people know when they are in trouble. The kind of trouble we are talking about here is information trouble. It centers around the support that a business must have to keep its sales or production going, and it has serious financial implications. For purposes of discussion we can group our troubles into those concerning time, money, and lack of information.

Time troubles show up in chronically late invoices and statements, backlogs of orders, excessive employee overtime, overdue reports, and the other kinds of nuisances that signal processing bottlenecks and inefficiencies. Bottlenecks cause problems in keeping up with current work. They also shut off the ability to expand.

Time troubles produce money troubles. Overtime is costly. Hiring more workers cuts into profits. As any business person will acknowledge, lost opportunity is very expensive. Often it's impossible to know the magnitude of such a loss.

Lack of information is much more insidious. So many business people try to make decisions without good, supporting information; for example, the way changes in costs affect profitability. The more volatile a business is, the more it needs timely information about its performance. Unfortunately, entrepreneurs in such businesses are the ones that are least likely to have the time to seek out good information systems.

The most common, nonautomated way to gather management information is to sit down with a calculator and a bunch of ledgers or reports and dig out the figures one is interested in. One problem with this method is that in order to arrange the numbers in different categories the tedious process must be repeated several times. For example, if you want to know profitability by salesperson by product, and then profitability by product by salesperson, you have to rearrange the same figures twice. Generally the business person is too busy or too turned off to ferret out this information, so he finds excuses for not having it. The classic excuse for not having timely information is that the business person knows by "experience" how the business runs.

While I do not argue that "gut feel" is a very important aid to the business person, relying on feelings rather than on accurate information does not maximize profits.

If the level of pain gets high enough, the business person recognizes that he's got to do something. Very often the idea of getting a computer occurs to him. Now he encounters a further dilemma. If he is not knowledgeable about computers, the fear of them can cause him to avoid pursuing what might just be the solution to his problems.

SYSTEMS ANALYSIS

The process of defining needs and finding automated solutions is called systems analysis. In complex business environments, a systems analyst is employed to evaluate needs and formulate solutions. He uses formal techniques and procedures to understand the way a business works and to document the changes that management wishes to make. In the small business environment, the owner or manager may wish to employ a consultant to help with systems analysis. While the project may not be so grand as designing and implementing a funds transfer system, the results of not understanding what the automation needs are and how to satisfy them properly can be very painful and expensive.

Objectives

What are the steps in the systems analysis process? In general, an analyst will start with a definition of the objectives and needs of the system, or in our case, of the business. A wholesaler's overall objective is to buy goods and resell them at a profit. Within this framework, he may have immediate objectives for improving the way he conducts his pursuit of profits. He may want to cut costs or increase capacity or reduce paper work. Perhaps the immediate objective is to get more accurate and timely information.

Scope

Once the needs and objectives have been determined, the scope of the project can be defined. Determining the scope of a project involves setting the boundaries within which change will take place. If the objective is to get the bills out faster, then the scope of the project will be limited to processing orders and producing invoices and statements. Payables and payroll activities will not be involved.

Current System

In order to determine change, the next step is to understand how the business currently operates. A careful study of current procedures and the data they act on is made. If a project is very broad in scope, such as automating an entire business, individual functions must be examined and detailed. The way each function relates to the others within the overall system must be defined and understood.

An example may illustrate how this works. Suppose we are analyzing a manufacturing concern that also wholesales its products. The initial part of this system concerns itself with all of the activities involved in manufacturing. Procedures include management of raw materials, scheduling and operating equipment at various work stations, managing employees' job assignments, and accounting for finished goods as they move into the sales function. The data falls into several categories including parts, workers' time, machine time, schedules, and finished products. This alone is a system in itself. Then the sales part of the business must be subjected to the same analysis in terms of its data and functions. After this, the interfaces between the two major areas must be determined. How are finished goods entered into inventory? How is the payroll handled? What are the various general ledger accounts and how are they affected by the different parts of the business? How are costs determined and allocated? How are profits determined and allocated? If the business is not currently automated, some more sophisticated functions such as cost accounting might not be included in the current system.

One of the best ways to find out how the current business works is to ask the people who are involved in the day-to-day operations. So many times the boss will decide what he thinks he needs without asking his employees for their valuable input. In an organization of any size, the boss does not usually know about the detailed routines that are performed. Employees are a wonderful source of information about inefficient forms, duplication of effort, bottlenecks in the processing flow, and so on. It should be mandatory to discuss plans for a computer system with one's employees. A side benefit of doing this up front is the incentive that an employee will have to learn the new system when he knows that he had a part in planning for it in the first place.

Once the current system is understood, it is then matched against the objectives, and alternatives for accomplishing the change are explored. It is prudent to do cost/benefit analyses on the various alternatives at this point. Here you will find out that the new system you thought you wanted will cost a quarter of a million dollars and require four more in staff and a new building. At this point you will probably reexamine your objectives. Perhaps you will find that there are some things you can live without.

Once a satisfactory alternative has been selected, it can be worked out in detail. A specification can be written listing all of the requirements for input, output, and data manipulation. If the requirements encompass many different functions, the project can be broken into phases. Perhaps the decision will be to automate order entry first. When that's working smoothly, receivables will be added. Later on other functions such as payables, payroll, and general ledger can be phased in.

As you can see, the analysis process concerns itself with understanding not only the various functions, but also the order in which they are performed. This helps to pinpoint the areas where change will affect the current work flow.

Perhaps the person who wrote up the orders will now be processing the invoices also, since the proposed system will produce them directly from the order information.

The analysis must consider the amount of data (how many orders) and the velocity at which the data flows through the business. (Are there busy times and slack times? How many transactions are processed hourly? Weekly? Monthly?) The magnitude and velocity of the data determine how powerful a system will be needed. They also determine how much media storage (such as disk) will be required, how many data entry terminals will be needed, and so on.

Availability of the system is another important factor. If the system must be working all the time, such as a 24-hour a day information service, then all components must be duplicated. Then, if one part fails, a switch can be made immediately to its backup. This is called "redundancy" in the system.

After the new system has been carefully specified, we enter the acquisition stage. Here is where we search out the software and hardware to satisfy our requirements.

SOFTWARE SOLUTIONS

When it comes to selecting a system for automating a business, software selection should be the first consideration. It is the logic of the programs that is ultimately going to satisfy the user's needs. Once the software is selected, the hardware on which it will run can be chosen. Sometimes hardware selection will be determined by the software that is chosen because the vendor has written the software for a particular computer. If we are selecting a generalized software package that has been designed to run on more than one computer, then we have more flexibility in our choice of hardware.

Packages

There are many good software packages on the marketplace for standard applications. This is particularly true of accounting software. The reasons for this are apparent. Accounting is governed by widely recognized rules which businesses adhere to. It is a relatively easy process, therefore, to write programs that will produce the mandated information that a business requires.

This is not to say that all business are alike. They certainly are not, and even if they have the same ultimate reporting requirements, the ways that firms conduct their business are many and varied. The preset logic and file structure in a particular accounting package may not fit your business' needs. Data base management packages that permit customized description and handling of data provide an alternative to specific software packages. In this way a business can use a standard tool to satisfy individualized requirements. If a business has relatively straightforward needs, it may be able to automate using one of the above solutions. The more popular software packages are generally available in several versions so that they will run on most popular hardware systems. Using a standard, off-the-shelf approach is by far the cheapest and safest solution to automation.

Custom Software

The opposite extreme to off-the-shelf software is software written specifically for one user. It meets the user's needs exactly. It is usually written by a programmer, either on the staff of the company or hired on a contract basis.

A nontechnical person will be at a disadvantage in evaluating whether or not the programs so developed are well written and efficient. He should be able to tell whether or not they produce the needed information.

The thing to understand in this situation is that needs are always changing. Once a program or set of programs is written, it must be maintained. Therefore, a business person must be willing to pay for ongoing programming support. In this respect, he is adding data processing to the list of functions in his business.

If the business is so far off the beaten track that standard software will not do the job, then custom programming may be the only alternative available. In this case, if the resulting system is modular and well documented, the business person may be able to generalize it a little and sell it to other users in the same field. At this point he is in the data processing business.

Customized Packages

This is the compromise solution for acquiring software. The user buys an existing package. Then he hires a programmer to modify it to meet certain needs that the original doesn't satisfy. This approach is usually cheaper than writing software from scratch. It has the added benefit of using the expertise of the vendor who created the original package. The user may discover functions which were not part of his original specification but which are very useful to him now that he knows about them. The downside risk is that the vendor may not support the package once it has been modified. Additionally, the user has the same problem assessing the expertise of the outside programmer he hires to make the modifications.

There is an alternative that we have not discussed yet that may be of interest to you if you have limited automation needs. On-line service bureaus will process your data on their computers. The way this works is as follows: you send them your order forms, payroll sheets, and so forth, and they enter the data into their computer and send you printed output. Alternatively, you can install one or more terminals in your location and link them to the service bureau's computer via telephone connections. Your employees enter the data which is then processed by the service bureau. You can get immediate on-line output on your terminal. Weekly and monthly reports are produced by the service bureau and sent to you. This is a very economical way to do a limited amount of computerization. The downside risk is that you have to accept the formats that the service bureau has set up, both for data entry and reports. Very little customization for your particular operation is available.

DOCUMENTATION

With any system that you purchase, quality documentation is vital. If your solution is to use various software packages, then you must have complete documentation for each one. Your employees are going to need good user manuals to learn how to run the individual programs that comprise your system. If you have customized any programs then you should insist on complete documentation of all changes. That way when you want to make further changes and the programmer who did your job is nowhere to be found, you will have a fighting chance to succeed. The new programmer should have a shot at understanding how the code works so that he doesn't mess things up too badly. If this sounds a little pessimistic, it is because we recommend that nontechnical people avoid custom solutions whenever possible. This is not to say that there are not some very fine programmers plying their talents. But how are you going to know the good ones from the bad ones?

HARDWARE SOLUTIONS

Once the software has been selected, the acquisition process moves on to hardware selection. Hardware systems may be very roughly categorized as:

Microcomputers	8- to 16-bit CPU	up to $ 40,000
Minicomputers	16- to 32-bit CPU	up to $200,000
Mainframes	32 bits +	over $200,000

These are admittedly very broad categories with tremendous overlap. This fact becomes painfully obvious when the search for hardware begins. It is vital to keep the user's requirements in mind so that one does not get sidetracked with issues like "newest," "most-powerful," and "fastest." You may not need the newest or the fastest.

There are certain factors that will determine the size, speed, and power of the required system. They are based on the user's input, processing, storage, and output needs and the state of the user's finances.

The amount of data that is input to the system and the locations that it is input from will determine whether or not a multiuser system with multiple input stations (keyboards and screens) is required. In configuring a system, enough resources must be available to handle peak periods in the work flow. If the business is cyclical, this means there will be times when some of the terminals and other resources will be idle. A multiuser system will require more memory than a single-user system. It will run faster if it has a more powerful CPU (Central Processing Unit). If there are remote locations then a communications capability will be required as well.

Storage capacity is determined by the amount of data that has to be available for access. For an order entry system, the entire customer file and product file must be accessible. If this is a large file, it would be foolish to store it on several floppy disks that would have to be switched constantly to update the proper accounts as the orders came in. In this case hard disk would be required to meet the user's needs. On the other hand, if the system is to be used for many small, unrelated jobs like creating word processing documents, floppy disk capacity might suffice. No business should consider purchasing a system with less than two floppy disk drives. Otherwise copying files is too tedious a process to be acceptable. If you plan to have hard disk on the system, then one floppy drive is sufficient.

The volume and quality of the output will determine the type of printer that is required. Letter quality printers are slow and expensive, but they are a must where the image of the company is represented by its correspondence. For internal reports inexpensive dot matrix printers will do fine.

Cost is obviously a factor. At this point it is important to realize the difference between a personal computer and a small business computer. A personal computer is a stand-alone, single-user system. This means only one person can use it at a time. Entry-level systems (those usually advertised in newspapers and magazines) have limited disk storage capacity and low cost printers (if a printer is included in the price at all). A very moderately priced personal computer such as the Apple, TRS-80, IBM Personal Computer, and others will be inadequate in business environments of any size. Therefore, a $5000 computer is probably not going to meet your needs as a small business person. On the other hand, machines in the upper end of the minicomputer range usually satisfy complex data processing requirements beyond the scope of our discussion. Using this definition, small business systems fall in the $15,000 to $100,000 range.

One very important factor to consider is the expandability of the system. Is it designed so that components can be easily added? Perhaps the current customer base is small and will fit on floppy disk. As the business grows more storage space will be needed and a hard disk will probably be required. Can one be added to the system without a hassle? Can more input stations, more memory, more printers be hooked up simply and easily? If a phased implementation is planned, it is particularly important to know how much horsepower is going to be required for each phase. In this way it may be possible to spread the cost of the final system over time by adding components only as they are needed.

SYSTEM SUPPORT AND SELECTION

There are several ways that small systems are sold. It is a rather confusing world for the prospective buyer. Things were much simpler when the vendor choices were limited to major mainframe and minicomputer companies. For these companies the price of a system is high enough to enable the vendor to provide support for the customer. Support includes customized demonstrations, on-site installation and training, customization of software, and on-going technical support. Therefore, the company is making a major investment in the sales, service, and technical support areas of its business.

This is not the case in the microcomputer world. In most cases the manufacturer does not sell directly to the consumer. There are distributors and dealers who sell the wares of various hardware and software companies. They range from very large wholesale operations to small mail-order houses. The level of support varies also, ranging from pretty good to nonexistent.

If you need a small business computer, however, dealing with a large vendor company is not always a benefit. Large companies are looking for large clients. The small business person very often gets short shrift from salespeople who do not see large commissions ahead. Service can also be a problem. Preferred customers get preferred treatment. Some companies have grown so quickly and have sold so many systems that they are not able to provide the level of service they would like to. On the other hand, a very nice feature that some companies offer is a "hot line." They provide the customer with a phone number to call for information and help. The phone is manned by people who are specially trained to answer your questions.

An alternative to consider is the OEM (Original Equipment Manufacturer). An OEM does not manufacture equipment, so the name is very misleading. An OEM adds value to a specific manufacturer's system. This usually takes the form of custom software which is packaged with the hardware and sold to the customer. OEMs usually have technical backgrounds. Often they are former employees of the companies whose hardware they are selling, particularly if it is a minicomputer. They install the hardware and the software and provide initial training in its use. After the break-in period they may or may not charge for additional training support. If they make changes to the software they are selling, the customer can acquire the upgrades. There may or may not be a charge for this. Bugs in the software, that is, errors on the vendor's part, are fixed free of charge. The only problem here would be purchasing a system from an OEM who subsequently goes out of business. Of course, major computer companies have also been known to go out of business, so there is no such thing as absolute security.

Another alternative is the private dealer who is selling one or more well known (and not so well known) computers. He usually sells standard software packages, too, so he can set you up with the hardware and software you need to do your job.

If you decide to purchase a system at a retail establishment, chances are you will get very little support. All you may get is a manual to lead you through a self-instruction course. In this situation, have a good look at the documentation and ask what kind of support the store provides. You can also check to see if any courses are offered by private companies, by consultants, or at local instructional facilities. If you are uneasy about diving in with nothing but a manual, a course might be the answer.

It is probably a good idea to say a few words about "salesman hype." If you are dealing with an established company, such as one of the well-known minicomputer manufacturers, the salesperson will probably know what he is talking about. The company has invested some time and money to train him, so he is knowledgeable about his product. He is probably not a technical person, but he does have a technical staff supporting him that he can call on to get answers for you. This is not the case in the microcomputer world. Here the range of expertise varies from marvelous (the ex-techie who went into business for himself) to horrendous (the local retail store that has to hire some "bodies" to fill up the space). If what the salesperson is saying doesn't make much sense to you, find another. Go someplace else if you can't get straight answers.

A word to the wise. Do not buy the first of anything, be it hardware or software, unless you are very adventurous. If the system is a good one, it will have satisfied users, and you will want to talk to one or two before you make your purchase. You should be able to get some references from the salesperson who is so anxious to sell you his system.

MAINTENANCE

You should have a maintenance agreement for your hardware. All computers have component failures from time to time. If you have a serious failure and have to replace something like the CPU board, you could wind up spending more than the cost of the maintenance agreement for one service call. If you are one of the fortunate few who never experiences a hardware failure, you can write the maintenance agreement off as guaranteeing your "peace of mind."

OBSOLESCENCE

Computer technology is changing very rapidly these days. We are constantly reading about the latest innovations in speed, size, and power. This very often leads the business person to want to wait so that he can buy the newest and best computer on the market. Thinking this way is a trap. No matter when one buys a computer, it will almost certainly be technologically obsolete in 12

to 15 months. We are speaking primarily of the hardware. Therefore, the business person must consider *functional* obsolescence when making his decision. At what point will the computer be unable to meet the needs of the business?

Though hardware changes very rapidly, software changes much more slowly. There is some comfort in this since it is the software that is the primary consideration in selecting a system. It may be as much as a year before there is a body of packaged software on the marketplace that will run on new hardware systems. The software designers and programmers must modify already existing programs to take advantage of the new hardware developments and this takes time. Therefore, business decisions should be made considering things like business growth. Will the system in mind be able to meet the anticipated needs caused by expansion, increases in volume, and so on? Changes of this type are usually changes in degree, not in kind. If the system was chosen with expansion in mind and was suited to the type of processing the business requires then it should meet those needs regardless of whether or not the hardware is the newest available. The planning horizon should then be the pay out period that justified the acquisition cost of the system in the first place. The business person can keep track of new developments in computer technology. He can then take advantage of newer technology in his next planning cycle when he needs to replace his current system.

There is never a case where all desires are perfectly satisfied. Even if everything is perfect at the moment of acquisition, new requirements pop up immediately. It is foolish to expect the perfect solution to your needs. On the other hand, you should not be satisfied with an inadequate system. Like so many other things, deciding on a computer system is a judgment call on the part of the business person. He is the one who has to decide how much he should compromise. The more knowledgeable he is about how computers work and what's available, the better able he is to make his decision.

CONSULTANTS

If you are unsure of what you need, whether a particular system will meet your needs or not, whether to get a computer at all, get some help. Even though consultant fees are not cheap in most cases, you can save a lot of time and aggravation by hiring a consultant to advise you. You can avoid a costly and painful mistake such as acquiring a system that won't do the job or being talked into a much larger system than your business requires.

2

Data

We begin our exploration of computers and their use in small business by looking at the information computers deal with. This is, of course, your information. You need to manage it in certain ways to know what's going on in your business. When you think about getting a computer, your basic reason is to improve the way you are going to manage your information.

Throughout this book we will be discussing what computers do with information and how they do it. First, though, we are going to look at some of the characteristics of the information itself. The reason we are doing this is that the information imposes certain demands and restrictions on computers that we want to understand. Later on we'll take a look at the construction and functioning of computers to understand the limitations on the information we can get out of them.

You will notice that we have been talking about information. At this point it is useful to introduce the term "data" and to make a distinction between data and information.

DATA AND INFORMATION

The dictionary defines data as: facts, information, statistics or the like, either historical or derived by calculation or experimentation. Not very helpful, is it? In this definition data and information are synonymous. The definition doesn't say anything about two very important features that distinguish between data and information. One is understandability, and the other is usefulness. Let us remove "information" from the definition of data. Let's define information as data that is both *understood by* and *useful to* human beings.

So often we represent facts and ideas, but nobody understands them. We are putting out data, but we don't have information.

Not having enough data and, therefore, lacking information is a serious problem. We do not have the basis for making proper decisions. Believe it or not, drowning in too much *data* is also a serious problem. We see this problem all the time in systems that produce too many reports or produce reports that are too detailed. We don't look at the output after the first time. We are too busy trying to do useful work. Of course we're being hampered in our efforts because we have data but not *information*. What we are going to be looking for, then, in future chapters, are systems that will provide us with the data that we need and that will let us organize it and get at it in convenient and understandable ways. Therefore, we need to keep our definition in mind as we get into the subject of what computers do with data because we are going to base our ultimate evaluations of worth on whether or not the data is useful to us.

APPLICATION TYPES

We are all constantly using data in both our business and personal lives. Such data has certain characteristics defined by our needs for it.

Business data is used to record transactions, store information about people and things, and keep track of financial matters. The characteristics of this data include documenting events and assuming financial responsibility. After all, buying goods, paying employees, and reporting income to the government all require that numbers be accurate and verifiable. Lest this seem overly simplistic, have a look at educational data for comparison purposes. The purpose of this kind of data is to instruct. It is full of descriptions and explanations. Very often we use pictures and other graphic representations to convey information. Scientific data is characterized by formulas, precise technical language, and numeric representations.

Why are we bothering with these different types of applications and their data? It is because the type of data we are using requires the computer to behave in certain ways to handle it. Business data requires a lot of input and output activity. We put information in about customers, products, orders, and the like. We file it in the computer, and then we get it out to produce shipping notices, invoices, statements, checks, reports, and so forth. Scientific data, on the other hand, does not usually have heavy input and output requirements. We enter a complex formula and ask the computer to massage it and tell us how much fuel we need to reach the moon. Our input may be one line and our output may be one number. In this case we need a computer that can handle very large numbers efficiently.

We've introduced the idea that different applications require data with different characteristics. Before we can pursue the relationship between our data and the way we use computers to produce it, we have to discuss some fundamentals about what data looks like from the computer's point of view.

DATA STRUCTURE IN THE COMPUTER

Computers do not understand things the way human beings do. We use symbols and language to represent facts and ideas. These symbols take many forms: pictures, numbers, letters and words, and so on. We need these symbols to transmit information among ourselves. Thus our language has very complex structures that let us store information and communicate it. Our thought processes interpret the words and symbols and produce some level of understanding. We deal with ambiguity and misunderstanding all the time. The computer cannot handle ambiguity.

The computer is a *binary* machine. It processes information based on certain characteristics of electricity: a switch is "on" or "off"; current is flowing or it isn't flowing; a field is magnetized in one direction or another direction. Since the computer consists basically of a series of binary storage units and switches connected by lines through which electricity flows, it is defined by its construction to be logically binary. We will get into how the computer manages these "on" and "off" conditions in Chapter 3 when we discuss hardware. Something that is either on or off, but not in both states at the same time, can be tested for its state. The result is known and, therefore, not open to interpretation. It is entirely unambiguous.

Bits and Bytes

For those of you who are not mathematicians, we're going to spend a few minutes on number systems so that we can understand the basis for data representation and manipulation in the computer.

All data in a business computer is represented by *bits*. A bit is the abbreviation for binary digit. Each bit takes up one place in the computer's storage schemes. A digit, as you know, is a number. The binary digits are 0 and 1. A binary number system has only two digits, and all quantities are represented by these two digits. By contrast, a decimal number system has ten digits, 0 through 9, an octal number system has eight digits, 0 through 7, and so on.

In order to represent a quantity greater than 1 in a binary system, we must position our digits to represent succeeding orders of magnitude. A binary number system is based on increasing powers of 2. Stated exponentially, $2^1 = 2$, $2^2 = 4$, $2^3 = 8$. A table of positions of binary digits with their corresponding decimal values is shown in Figure 2.1.

Position								
9	8	7	6	5	4	3	2	1
Power of 2								
2^8	2^7	2^6	2^5	2^4	2^3	2^2	2^1	2^0
Decimal value								
256	128	64	32	16	8	4	2	1

Let's see how we represent numbers using this scheme. Since we have only two digits, we represent the number 3 (in decimal) as 11. We have a 1 in the 2^0 column and a 1 in the 2^1 column. If we add the values of these two columns together we get $2 + 1 = 3$.

Let's try something a little harder. What would 1011 be in decimal?

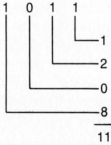

Adding from left to right across the columns of our table we have $8 + 2 + 1 = 11$. We don't add in the value for 2^2 because we have a 0 in that position.

There are a couple of interesting things one can do with a binary number system. If we group a series of three binary positions together, we get an octal number system or base 8 system. In this system there are eight digits, 0 through 7. Sample numbers look like this:

Binary	Octal
001	1
101	5
001 101	15

If we group a series of four binary digits together we get a hexadecimal number system. Hexadecimal means base 16, so there are 16 digits in this system. In order to represent digits above 9 in the units position, we add six letters, A, B, C, D, E, and F. The decimal number 11, which is our old friend 1011 in binary, would be B in hexadecimal. (See Appendix C.)

The convenient grouping of binary numbers makes our job of dealing with computers a little easier. As we have said, the only thing the computer understands is 0 or 1.

000111100111 is an impossible symbol for a person to deal with. 1E7 is a little easier for us to understand. I realize this may all seem a little confusing to you right now. We will deal with the translation from machine language, which is the 0s and 1s we've been talking about, to higher level languages when we talk about software in Chapter 4. One more note, however. You will notice that a decimal number base is not a natural form for a computer to deal with. There is no power of 2 that gives us a base 10 system. Unfortunately, you cannot pay your employees in hexadecimal. So hardware and software solutions have

Figure 2.2 Reprinted courtesy of Jack Schmidt.

been developed to convert the binary data in the computer to decimal and other forms.

You can believe that even though the computer can understand only a series of 0s and 1s, human beings have been clever enough to figure out that binary computerese can be used to represent other forms of data. So far we have been translating direct numeric values between binary and decimal number bases. The computer can also represent alphabetic data. Let's go on with our discussion to see how we represent character data.

You've probably stumbled on the term *byte* in your reading. A byte is 8 bits. It is the primary form of representing characters in a computer today. Earlier computers dealt in aggregations of 6 or 7 bits, but today the byte is the standard. The numbers and letters that human beings use are represented in the computer with 8 bits. There are 256 possible values for 8 bits (0 to 255). You can see this by looking back at the positional chart and noticing that if we put a 1 in every position from 2^0 through 2^7 we'd get 255 in decimal. Since we only have 26 letters in our alphabet and nine digits, we have lots of values left over for special symbols and codes to tell the computer special things. There are standards for the meanings of the various values and, therefore, the bit combinations that form characters. One of them is ASCII, American Standard Code for Information Interchange. Most microprocessor-based computers today use the ASCII values for character representation. Figure 2.3 shows the representation of the ASCII character set.

Fields, Records, and Files

We are fast approaching things that human beings can deal with. We collect our characters into groups and they become words and numbers that have meaning for us. We call these words and numbers *fields*. If we are dealing with employee payroll information, for example, last name would be a field, first name would be another field. The amount of salary would be another field, as would be the number of exemptions.

Once we have all of the information about an employee that we need for the payroll, we put it together in a *record*. Records of all of the employees for the company are grouped together in a *file* or data set. We can have different files for different purposes, such as accounts receivable, accounts payable, and general ledger. Some purposes can require more than one file. For example, in order to process our receivables, we may need a customer file, a product file, an order file, an invoice file, and a payment file.

ASCII Characters and Decimal Values.
The following table lists computer definable characters according to their "decimal" value.

Decimal	Character	Decimal	Character	Decimal	Character
0	CTRL-@	44	,	88	X
1	CTRL-A	45	—	89	Y
2	CTRL-B	46	.	90	Z
3	CTRL-C	47	/	91	LEFT BRACKET
4	CTRL-D	48	0	92	BACKSLASH
5	CTRL-E	49	1	93	RIGHT BRACKET
6	CTRL-F	50	2	94	UP ARROW
7	CTRL-G	51	3	95	UNDERLINE
8	CTRL-H	52	4	96	GRAVE
9	TAB/CTRL-I	53	5	97	a
10	CTRL-J	54	6	98	b
11	CTRL-K	55	7	99	c
12	CTRL-L	56	8	100	d
13	RETURN	57	9	101	e
14	CTRL-N	58	:	102	f
15	CTRL-O	59	;	103	g
16	CTRL-P	60	LESS THAN	104	h
17	CTRL-Q	61	=	105	i
18	CTRL-R	62	GREATER THAN	106	j
19	CTRL-S	63	?	107	k
20	CTRL-T	64	@	108	l
21	CTRL-U	65	A	109	m
22	CTRL-V	66	B	110	n
23	CTRL-W	67	C	111	o
24	CTRL-X	68	D	112	p
25	CTRL-Y	69	E	113	q
26	CTRL-Z	70	F	114	r
27	ESC	71	G	115	s
28	FS	72	H	116	t
29	GS	73	I	117	u
30	RS	74	J	118	v
31	US	75	K	119	w
32	SPACE	76	L	120	x
33	!	77	M	121	y
34	"	78	N	122	z
35	#	79	O	123	LEFT BRACE
36	$	80	P	124	VERTICAL LINE
37	%	81	Q	125	RIGHT BRACE
38	&	82	R	126	TILDE
39	'	83	S	127	DEL/RUBOUT
40	(	84	T		
41	)	85	U		
42	*	86	V		
43	+	87	W		

The standard printing characters fall between 32 and 126. Control characters fall between 0 and 31.

Figure 2.3 ASCII character set.

Data Bases

We need to introduce the concept of a "program" at this point. A *program* is a series of instructions that tells the computer how to handle data. It is the way we cause the computer to act logically. Programs contain the logic to perform arithmetic, comparison, and storage functions on data.

Early computer programs dealt with data in the file structure we have just been discussing. Programs contained the logic to act upon the data in the fields within the records within the files. The programs and the files were stored together. Programs had their own files, so to speak. Many systems still use this data structure. Problems started to develop, however, when we needed the same piece of data for more than one program or set of programs. Not only did the payroll program need the employee's name and address, but also the benefits program and the medical program and the tuition assistance program needed it. What happened when the employee moved? If each program had its own separate file, then the change of address had to be processed separately for each one. Needless to say, the chances of missing the change in one or two of the files was very good. So we began to realize that redundant data storage was inefficient and difficult to maintain reliably.

If we separate the data from the program and store it in its own place, we can let more than one program get at it, and we have to worry about maintaining it only once. Everybody now has the latest version of the information.

Data bases also permit us to get at data at the field level. We can put all of the information about the employee in one place, but the payroll department has to deal with only the fields it needs. It can skip over the medical history that only the medical department is interested in. Since both departments need name and address, that data is available to both of them.

Additionally, if the personnel department wants a special report, the data processing staff can write programs to pick out the particular data needed even though it might originate in several other departments. Because all information is pooled in a central place, the programmers know what is available. There are some catches, though.

Data bases must be controlled and managed. Someone must be an administrator to make important decisions. What data are we going to store? If we compute a certain field, such as gross salary, by multiplying hours worked by rate of pay, do we have to keep the result? We can always go back and recompute it. What structure are we going to impose on the data so that we can establish how fields are related to each other? This is a very controversial topic in current data base systems. Name and address might be related to a lot of things, but level of education doesn't seem to be very important when we are looking for fields related to the payroll. If we are going to let many different programs access a common data base, then we have to understand which pieces of data the different programs need. At the same time we have to have an overall view of the total data needs of all of the programs so that we can include everything we need in the data base. We don't want to duplicate data items, however. We want to define and store a particular item only once. This is our old name and address problem.

Security is another concern for data base management. Who should be allowed to access the data? After all, if it's all in one place, some of it might be confidential, and we can't let unauthorized eyes see parts that are none of their business.

What about the correctness of the data that we change? How do we guard against one program putting in erroneous amounts, for example, that mess things up for everybody else?

As you can see, data bases introduce a certain complexity that requires a high level of skill to manage. There are complicated decisions to be made in the original design and establishment of a data base. The on-going maintenance and administration of the data base require trained personnel. Generally, large companies with large computers are most interested in establishing data bases. However, data base management packages are emerging for the small computer marketplace, so it is important to understand the distinction between them and traditional file structures. We will be talking more about data bases in Chapter 4.

DATA ACCESS

Interactive Mode

Interactive data use means that we are carrying on a dialogue with the computer. We fill in the blanks on an order, or, perhaps, we select a choice from a menu of activities. In other words, we sit at a keyboard or some other input device and enter information into the computer. The computer, doing its part, acknowledges the receipt of the data by showing that the blanks are filled in on the screen, or it displays the next screenful of instructions or blanks because it has accepted the previous one. We get immediate gratification in interactive mode because we can see the results of our actions. Things are happening in "real time." As is usually the case with computer jargon, the term real time can be puzzling to human beings. Think of it as real "human" time. Things are happening right now as we are experiencing them. Unfortunately, in interactive mode we are slowing the computer down to human speeds, which is incredibly slow as you will discover when we talk later on about the billionths of a second the computer really needs to do its work.

We have systems called single-user and multiuser systems. Single-user means that the data can be used by only one person at a time. For example, if a business has a computer with one screen and one keyboard, one operator can use its programs at a time. If the system can be used by several people at once, for example, if the computer has four screens and four keyboards, then it is a multiuser system.

Sometimes we want to share interactive data among users who have separate computers. In this case we have to link the computers somehow so that they can communicate with each other. We can use the telephone lines, or we can wire our computers together privately if they're close together.

Batch Mode

Another way that we can process data in a computer is in *batch* mode. In this mode the data is already collected on a diskette or a tape cassette, and we simply turn the computer loose on it. We run the payroll program, for example. Let us assume that we have already loaded information about each employee and his hours and rate of pay and whatever else is required into the computer. The computer can now use the logic in its programs to compute the salary for each employee and even print paychecks, if so desired.

Data used in batch mode is usually accessed *sequentially* by the computer. The information is organized in order, by employee number, perhaps, or alphabetically by last name. The computer reads through the information, starting at the beginning of the list of employees and processes each record without any outside help from human beings. When it reaches the end of the list, it is finished.

Sometimes we collect batches of data and then send them over telephone lines to another computer for further processing. We are still processing data in batch mode at the receiving end. This type of data handling is called *RJE,* which stands for Remote Job Entry.

The need to access data randomly or sequentially dictates the way we store it and the media we use to store it in. We will be discussing hardware in the next chapter, but for now I would like to mention that magnetic tape and tape cassettes are sequential media for storing information. You have to start at the beginning of the reel and read in sequence to find the information you want. Disks and diskettes, on the other hand, can be used both sequentially and randomly. Because they have tracks like phonograph records, the arm can be positioned over the particular track that has the information we want, or we can "play the whole record" sequentially.

Keys

The piece of data that we organize by is called the *key.* This is a very important concept in data access. We can use more than one key if we need a finer organization. For example, we organize our product file by type of product. Calculators might be one of our products. We then secondarily key by model if we carry several models of calculators.

When we use data interactively, we need to get at a particular employee or a particular product. In this case we access data *randomly.* Here is where the key comes in particularly handy. It lets us go directly to the customer or product we are looking for instead of having to start at the beginning of the information to read through all of it until we come to the record we want.

Another benefit is that we can compare against the key when we are adding new data to avoid duplication. Perhaps you are thinking, "Well, what about two employees with the name of Jones?" You are absolutely right. If all the computer compared on was "Jones," we wouldn't be able to tell which one was the vice-president of marketing and which one was the order entry clerk. Therefore it is essential that we use enough fields or that the fields be one of a kind so that we have a *unique key* for differentiating and locating data. In our present case we would have to include first name and middle initial in our key at a minimum. You can see why we are fast becoming a nation of walking social security numbers.

THE DATA PROCESSING CYCLE

We have been talking about data and its characteristics. In our discussion we have mentioned people entering data into the computer and looking at reports coming out of the computer. As you realize, most business data is dynamic. If we don't change it, or worse yet, if we want to change it and can't, then we lose the ability to record our business activity. Living data needs to be used and massaged.

The data processing cycle consists of three steps or activities that are performed on data. They are: *input, processing,* and *output.*

Input

First of all, we have to get the data into the computer. Most business data is created at a keyboard of some kind. Today we most often enter data directly into the computer. In earlier times keypunch operators punched the data onto punch cards which were then gathered together and fed into the computer in batch mode. Now we have many examples of direct data entry. Clerks at automated cash registers enter our purchases directly into computers. We enter our own data when we use automated tellers to do our banking transactions, and, of course, office workers capture business data at terminals.

There are other ways to capture data electronically. Optical Character Readers (OCRs) can be hooked up to computers. These machines scan printed material and translate the data into computer format. There are OCR devices that read handwritten data. The New York State Motor Vehicle Department uses such forms for drivers' licenses and vehicle registration. They have places to write in certain numeric changes like zip code which can be scanned by a computer. There are even computers that can recognize voice input, although this technology is in its infancy.

By contrast, a great deal of scientific data is captured by machines that are monitoring processes or even other machines. Very often the machines doing the monitoring contain computers themselves.

This brings us to an interesting problem about inputting data. If you have a machine creating data, then the data should be accurate unless the machine has some kind of mechanical malfunction. This is not true when you have human beings inputting data. Unfortunately, they make mistakes. They also change their minds. Computers must be programmed to accommodate these human frailties. Therefore, the editing capabilities of programs that accept data are very important to consider when we are evaluating programs. We need to catch errors like letters in a field that should only have dollars and cents, for example. We also need to be able to change our minds and reenter data if we make a mistake. On the other hand, we must be required to enter all the essential data for a particular transaction. A system that lets us bill a customer without requiring that we enter what he bought would not produce very good information.

Processing

We have to add information most of the time. We have new customers and new orders coming in if things are going well. So we must be able to easily accommodate new information. We need to know how the file or data base is structured. Sequential files must be resorted in order to keep the records in order. For random files we solve this problem by using an index. An index stores the address, or location, of the record in a file along with the data field which is the key. All we have to do is sort the keys. When we look up the key, the associated record number lets us retrieve the record we are looking for. In this way we can add records anywhere in the file as long as we keep our keys in order.

Sorting is a significant function on a computer and is one of the things that is so nice about machine manipulation of data. Since we can sort data in different sequences by using different keys, we can restructure information easily without having to input raw data each time we want a new report. Very often we use the sort and merge functions together. If we have a list of parts to add to our inventory file, for example, instead of adding them to the file one at a time, which is time consuming, we can enter all the new parts, sort them in order and then merge them into the master inventory file in sequence.

Of course we have to change data from time to time. We've already discussed updating names and addresses, for example.

Another function we have to perform is deletion. This is not as simple as it sounds. In some financial systems, in fact, once data is entered it cannot be deleted. In order to fix errors, new transactions are entered that adjust the previous amounts. This guards against tampering with the books. There is a record of each transaction so you know if a mistake was made, and if so, how it was fixed. In some systems, on the other hand, at the end of a financial period, or after data has been released to other programs, it is automatically deleted.

Output

Believe it or not, it's much easier to get data out of a computer than it is to put it in. I am assuming, of course, that we have well-written programs that produce reliable data. Depending on whether we just want to have a look at a particular piece of information or whether we want a permanent record to give to someone, we have some options for output. We can display the information on a screen device. This is good for small amounts of data. Screen devices usually display between one-half and one page of data at a time.

Here we are dealing with the computer in interactive mode. We need information immediately and temporarily. After we have retrieved the information and viewed it, we go on to the next set of information and replace what we have finished with.

We can print data on continuous forms or on single sheets of paper. We call this "hard copy." There are many needs for hard copy including reports, invoices, paychecks, letters, legal documents, and mailing labels.

Other forms of computer output include sound (both voice and music), microfilm, and magnetic disks and tapes. We will talk more about disks, diskettes, and tapes in the next chapter. Actually, these are both input and output media since the computer can store information on them and then retrieve it for further processing.

Transactions

Data that is transmitted between computers connected by telephone lines enters the receiving computer in "transactions." The message, or transaction, can contain a request for information from the receiving computer's files, or it can contain information that will change the existing files. The same thing happens, of course, when an operator enters transactions at a terminal directly connected to the computer. Transactions constitute a strange kind of data. They represent data in transition. This kind of data is different from data that is stored in a file or data base. Transactions can affect many different files. Therefore, we must manage transactional data. We must be able to add transactions, delete them, modify them, and store them. Transactions arrive in random order, so we have to keep track of them somehow. Generally what we do is to assign a sequence number to each transaction as it arrives. We also store transactions in a "log file" so that we know we got them. In case of errors, we can go back and look up the actual message that came in. We can find the transactions because we store the transaction number in the record when we update our data files with the new information that came in via the transaction. Sometimes we use a simple mechanism like the date to identify transactions.

DATA STORAGE

We mentioned early in this chapter that different types of data are used for different purposes. Business data records facts that we need to run the business. Some of the data carries financial responsibility. There is data that does not carry such responsibility. Letters and memos, for example, are informative, but we don't have the same worries about accuracy with them. We must determine how important our data is and how expendable it is. We will have to store some of it for a long time, and some of it we can discard pretty quickly. How long do we have to keep a log of our transactions, for example, once we have processed all our new orders and sent out our invoices?

On the other hand, some data is so critical that we take pains to "back it up." We make duplicate copies on disks or tapes so that we will always be in business in case something happens to the original files. Backup is especially important for peace of mind when dealing with computers. Even though today's computers are pretty reliable on the whole, they do fail occasionally. If we know that we have another copy of the general ledger, then we don't have to worry about going back to manual records or previous printouts to reenter all the data again.

There are several options as to where we store our data. We have a central data base option which we discussed previously. All of the businesses' data is in one data base and all of the programs access the data base. Integrated accounting programs running on microprocessor-based systems manage data this way. We could have several input stations or even several computers accessing a central data base.

In contrast to storing data centrally, sometimes it is more efficient to break it up. In this case, each department or unit can handle its own data. Transactions are input to computers assigned to the individual operating units. There has to be a common description of the data, however, if it is to be aggregated to produce company-wide information. There also has to be some central collecting mechanism to produce the "aggregate."

A third alternative is stand-alone data in separate files. We may not need lots of input stations or computers. If we simply want to use a computer for one purpose, like word processing, or to do some personal business and perhaps, to play a few games, separate files are appropriate.

We have now completed our exploration of data. We know something about its characteristics, how we represent it in the computer, how we manipulate and store it, and some of the challenges it presents for computers. We looked at small business computing from the viewpoint of the data to gain a global perspective on information. We did this before we got enmeshed in the technical details of the hardware and software which often tend to obscure the larger business purposes which brought us to an investigation of computers in the first place. We are now ready to further our knowledge base by exploring the theoretical and actual ways that computers work.

3

Hardware

Our discussion now takes us to an exploration of the technical aspects of a computer, into the worlds of *hardware* and *software*. By hardware we mean the physical components of the computer, such as the screen, keyboard, disk, printer, memory, and central processing unit.

The logic that causes the hardware to function in certain ways is software. Programmers write software to perform two major functions:

1   to direct the activities of the hardware (operating systems and other system software),
2   to manipulate data to produce information (applications software).

In this chapter we will discuss hardware, and we will explore software in Chapter 4.

This discussion is designed to give you basic information about how a computer works. The emphasis will be on microcomputers.

HISTORY OF THE COMPUTER

Man has devised various methods for counting over time. Starting with the most basic instruments, his fingers, he has ingeniously evolved more and more complex tools and systems. The latest development is a mind-boggling tool which many feel defies understanding, the computer.

Whether they used stones, notched sticks, sand drawings, or some other form of positional notation, early counting systems were primarily decimal and manual. The abacus is, of course, one of the first counting machines to come to mind. It dates back before 500 B.C. The "modern version" was developed about 200 A.D.

With the development of writing materials, counting could be recorded. The documentation of business transactions supported the growth of government and commerce, and so the demand for computation grew. Eventually people began to think of ways to relieve the boring work of computing numbers by hand.

In 1642 Blaise Pascal invented an automatic, mechanical calculator. It used wheels that were precisely interconnected by gears. When each wheel completed one revolution, it shifted its neighboring wheel one-tenth of a revolution. The "Pascaline" could only perform addition and subtraction. It was not widely accepted, due in part to some mechanical shortcomings and in part to the same kind of fear and anxiety about machines that is expressed about computers today.

A major advance in mechanical calculation occurred later in the seventeenth century when Gottfried Leibniz perfected a calculating machine that not only added and subtracted, but also multiplied, divided, and extracted square roots. He improved upon Pascal's device by adding a stepped cylinder that represented the digits 1 through 9. This was known as the Leibniz wheel.

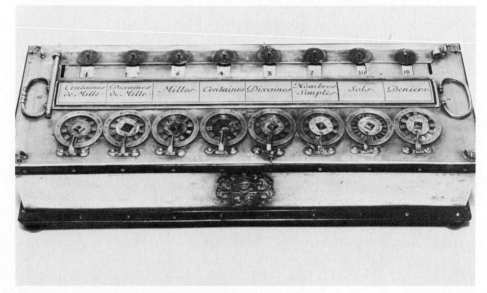

Figure 3.1 The Pascaline, courtesy of IBM.

Thus, in 1673 bookkeepers and mathemeticians had a general-purpose calculating machine to ease the drudgery of writing numbers. This calculator was widely used in Leibniz's time.

Leibniz made another important contribution that was to prove fundamental to the modern concept of computers. It was in the field of symbolic logic. He was far ahead of his time in the formulation of such principals as logical addition, logical multiplication, and negation. It would take another century before these ideas would be formalized in algebraic notation by George Boole.

One of the great names in the history of computers is that of Charles Babbage. He was another genius ahead of his time. Although he was never able to complete a working model of his Difference Engine or his Analytic Engine, he conceived in them most of the essential features of modern-day digital computers. The Analytic Engine was divided into two parts, the "mill," which performed arithmetic processes, and the "store," which contained data to be worked on and which stored intermediate results. The control of the process was based upon the use of punched cards similar to those used in the Jacquard weaving loom. A major feature of the Analytic Engine was its ability to make conditional jumps. This meant that the order of instructions could be modified so that it would be possible to return to a previous point and repeat a sequence several times. In modern computerese we call this a "loop." Because Babbage was working in the 1830s and 1840s, the mechanical capabilities to implement

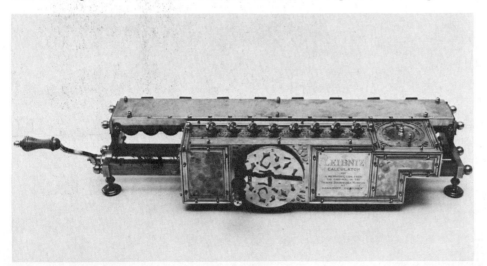

Figure 3.2 The Leibniz calculator, courtesy of IBM.

his ideas did not yet exist. Consequently his life was a series of frustrations and disappointments. His ideas would, however, be incorporated in the early computers of the twentieth century.

While all of the mechanical breakthroughs were very important to its development, we would not have the modern binary version of the computer without the genius of George Boole. In 1854 he published *The Laws of Thought, on which are founded the Mathematical Theories of Logic and Probabilities.* Here was the formulation of Boolean algebra, a system of symbolic logical notation that recognizes three basic operations, AND, OR, and NOT. The design and operation of modern computers is based on the symbolic logic of Boolean algebra. Since Boolean rules deal with two states, that is, true and false, electronic circuits can be constructed to perform logically according to them. The "on" or "off" states, that is, current flowing through a switch or not flowing through a switch correspond to true and false conditions. We will explore this concept in greater detail a little later in this chapter.

As the Industrial Revolution brought us into the twentieth century, there were increasing demands for machines to process information more quickly and efficiently. In 1890 Herman Hollerith developed a machine that read punched cards. It was used to tabulate the census results. It replaced the manual effort of thousands of clerks whose efforts would have produced results

Figure 3.3 Reconstruction of Babbage's difference engine, courtesy of IBM.

about the time the 1900 census was due to be taken. As a result of using Hollerith's machine, the 1890 census figures were available in two and one-half years. Punched cards became the first mass medium for entering data into a computer. Hollerith's company was eventually to evolve into that well-known giant of the computer industry, IBM.

Once the mechanical and logical foundations were laid, further theoretical work advanced the cause of computers in the first half of the twentieth century. Alan Turing made an important contribution to computing theory by postulating that one machine could be *programmed* to imitate another machine. This created the notion of a universal machine whose logic could be duplicated in any other like machine. Building upon this work, von Neumann and others realized that a computer could store a program to be used to direct its activities. This was a breakthrough from the early programming of computers which required that the logic be loaded into the machine by setting switches by hand. Once the logic was set, it could not be modified while the program was running. With the discovery that programs could be stored in the computer and their logic accessed the same way that data was stored and accessed, computers could be designed for generalized functions. Sequences could be selected and modified dynamically according to the logic contained in the program. Babbage was finally vindicated.

World War II created large-scale information needs. In 1944, Howard Aiken, working for the Navy, led the project that developed the Automatic Sequence Controlled Calculator, commonly known as Mark I. It was 51 ft. long and 8 ft. high. It contained about 800,000 parts and over 500 miles of wire. It could handle numbers to 23-decimal-digit positions and could perform additions in 0.3 sec. It used electromechanical relays for its switching logic, and it performed decimal arithmetic. Mark I was big, hot, and slow, but it was much faster than human beings.

In 1937 C. E. Shannon, a graduate student at MIT, discovered the logical connection between Boole's symbolic logic and the switching capability of electromechanical relays. The logical compatibility of electronic circuits and binary calculation was now established. Although some early computers worked in decimal, computer designers eventually realized that a binary approach was natural to a computer and that a decimal design was not.

The world's first commercially produced electronic digital computer was completed in 1951. Called Univac I, it was the brain child of J. P. Eckert, Jr. and John Mauchly. Previous advances by these two men included the replace-

Figure 3.4 Mark I, courtesy of IBM.

ment of electromechanical relays with vacuum tubes and the use of stored programs (Eniac), as well as the use of magnetic tapes instead of punched cards
and the use of an all-binary system (Binac). In addition to these advances, Univac I used a compiler to translate programs into computer machine language.
We will talk more about programs and compilers in Chapter 4.

TRANSISTORS

Now the world waited for the development of the transistor to move into the
modern computer era. It was discovered at Bell Labs in 1948. A transistor is
a tiny electronic switch made from semiconductor material. Semiconductors
slow down the current flow so that it can be controlled more easily. Since transistors have no moving parts, the use of them is called solid-state technology.
     One type of transistor is made in a layering process in which a semicon-

ductor material (the substrate) is "doped" or infused with tiny regions of a different type of semiconductor material. Current will flow easily through the same type of material. One type insulates the other type, however, impeding current flow. An insulating layer of glass (silicon oxide) is applied to the semiconductor layer. Holes are made through the insulating layer by using a mask to determine where the exposed areas of the semiconductor layer should be. The areas are to act as switches. Again, a masking process is used to apply regions of metal to the switch areas. The metal connects the tiny regions across the substrate. This process produces a MOS (Metal-Oxide Semiconductor) transistor. When a transistor is active, a voltage is applied to the metal gate to close the switch and permit current to flow between the regions of like semiconductor material that are insulated by the substrate. The combination of many transistors on one chip is called an Integrated Circuit (IC) chip. If negative material is doped into a positive substrate, we have NMOS chips. If positive material is doped into a negative substrate, we have PMOS chips. A combination of the two is call CMOS. CMOS uses the least amount of electrical current for its operation.

Integrated circuit chips are roughly 1/4 in. square. They are manufactured from silicon crystals which are grown commercially and then sliced. A slice is 3 to 4 in. in diameter and about one-hundredth of an inch thick. In order to make chip production commercially feasible, large quantities of chips are produced using masks which repeat the chip logic many times. This process creates hundreds of the same type of chip on the surface of the slice of silicon.

Once the chips are created, they are cut up and packaged in Dual In-Line Packages (DIPs). The DIP is sometimes mistakenly referred to as a chip. In fact, it contains the wires that connect the chip to the external pins on the DIP. The DIP plugs in to the board which has wires printed on it. (See Figure 3.15.) In this way the tiny circuits on the chip are wired together so that the signals can be sent via the board to specified wires of other chips throughout the computer.

Circuit designers plan the functions of a chip. They design circuit logic and then use photographic techniques to reduce the plans to microscopic size. Masks are produced from the plans to be used in the layering process described above. The fewer the number of masks and the fewer the number of layering processes, the cheaper it is to make transistors. As the techniques for miniatur-

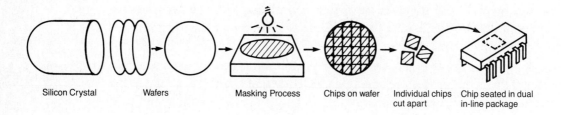

Silicon Crystal   Wafers   Masking Process   Chips on wafer   Individual chips cut apart   Chip seated in dual in-line package

Figure 3.5 Chip creation process.

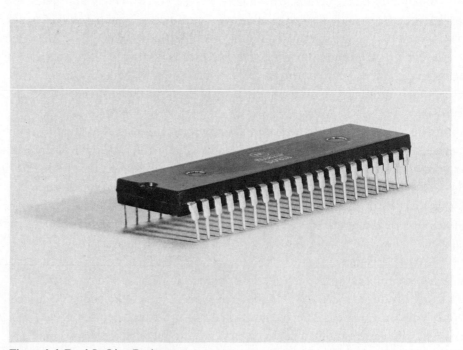

Figure 3.6 Dual In-Line Package.

ization improve, we are able to pack more and more circuits on an individual chip. This means more and more functions can be provided in smaller and smaller spaces. SSI (Small-Scale Integration) chips of the early 1960s contained 10 to 12 logic gates. MSI (Medium-Scale Integration) chips contained up to 1000 gates, and LSI (Large-Scale Integration) chips moved from that number to 50,000 gates per chip. VLSI (Very Large-Scale Integration) ranges over 100,000 gates per chip. ELSI (Extremely Large-Scale Integration) is under development now.

Chips are designed to perform different functions. The most common chips are memory chips, peripheral control chips, and Central Processing Unit chips (CPU). The most complicated of these chips is the CPU chip.

The semiconductor market has been experiencing phenomenal growth during the last few years. Sales were about $13.6 billion in 1980. By 1985 estimates suggest they will be $38 billion.

BINARY LOGIC

The modern computer is a binary machine. Its basic building block, the transistor, performs two functions: (1) it acts as a switch to pass or inhibit the flow of electricity; (2) it stores a charge to indicate an "on" or "off" condition. Why are these two functions important?

All data storage, computations, and logical operations are accomplished in the computer by recognizing an "on" or "off" condition. We store data as a series of 0s and 1s, as we mentioned in Chapter 2. We must also manipulate the data. For this we need to apply logic (programs) to data. Programs are also stored in the computer in bits. Specific bit combinations represent instructions. The instructions are decoded by combinations of transistors which send signals along to activate other transistors. This process ripples through the computer accomplishing such tasks as reading data from a keyboard device, performing calculations, and writing data to a disk file. All of these activities happen because we can combine the AND, OR, and NOT logical functions to produce a given signal on a given line at a given time.

We can represent AND logic in an electrical circuit by hooking up a couple of switches in a series to light a light bulb. In order for the light to shine, both switches must be closed.

We can show OR logic by connecting our switches in parallel. Since the

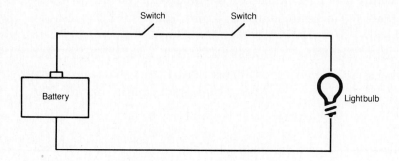

Figure 3.7 AND circuit logic.

electricity generated by the battery now has two paths by which it can reach the light bulb, closing one of the switches will activate the bulb. The tiny transistors in a computer perform this switching function and permit the accomplishment of logical operations.

Transistors that have been connected in logical patterns are called logic gates. The major types of gates are AND gates, OR gates, and NOT gates (inverters) corresponding to the major Boolean operators. By combining AND and NOT logic we get the NAND gate and likewise, by combining OR and NOT logic we get the NOR gate. I mention these last two gates because an entire CPU can be made by using just one or the other.

These gates are called *combinational* circuits. Signals arrive on their input lines and are combined according to the logic they represent so that the

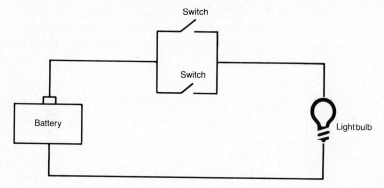

Figure 3.8 OR circuit logic.

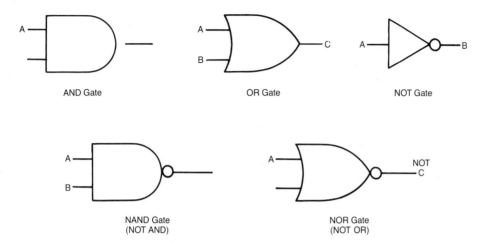

Figure 3.9 Logic gate symbols.

appropriate output is produced. Among other things, we use combinational circuits to create adders so we can do binary calculations, to make decoders that can convert binary numbers to octal or hexadecimal equivalents, and to make multiplexers that select one bit from a large number of bits to enable certain functions. All of these functions and many more are required for the computer to do its work. There is a problem with combinational circuits, however. They do not store information. They just act upon the input to produce immediate output.

FLIP-FLOPS

There are times when the computer has to remember information so that it can be acted upon later. For this purpose we need *sequential* logic circuits. The most basic sequential logic building block is the flip-flop. It can be made from two NAND gates. One output line from each gate is criss-crossed back to become an input to the other gate. Schematically a simple flip-flop looks like this:

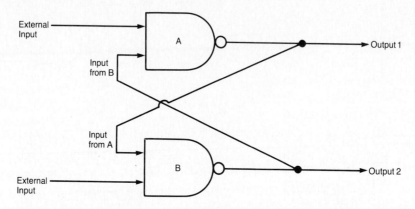

Figure 3.10 Flip-flop.

Flip-flops are used in various combinations for registers, memories, counters and in other functional areas where the computer must hold on to information for a while before it is used.

Now that we have discussed the theoretical foundations for a computer, let's look at how theory has been translated into function.

HARDWARE FUNCTIONAL GROUPINGS

Hardware may be generally grouped into three functional areas:

1. The central processing unit (CPU).
2. Memory.
3. Input and output.

Sets of wires, called buses, connect the components of these three groupings and enable the transfer of information by the computer. Their logical functions are to carry data, addresses, and control information between the CPU and internal memory or external devices.

THE CENTRAL PROCESSING UNIT (CPU)

The central processing unit or CPU is the heart of the computer. In microcomputers its functions are usually performed by one IC chip. This chip is responsi-

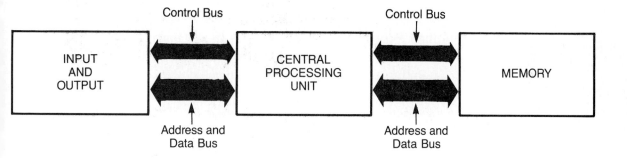

Figure 3.11 Hardware functional groups.

ble for executing program instructions, reading data in and writing data out, and controlling the operation of the computer in an orderly fashion.

Microprocessor chips began their history in 1969. Early work led to the development of a 4-bit chip to perform arithmetic and logic functions in programmable calculators. With the advent of the 8-bit chip, the microprocessor market took off. By the mid-1970s more than 50 companies were in the chip business. By "8-bit" chip we mean the capacity of the chip to handle 8 bits as a unit. We call this the *word length*. A commonly accepted distinction between a microcomputer and a minicomputer is the chip bit width. Minicomputers typically have 16-bit CPU chips. These distinctions are blurring rapidly, however. Several companies have recently introduced 32-bit chips at the minicomputer level, among them Digital Equipment Corporation and Data General. The 16-bit chip is finding its way into the microprocessor market in the IBM Personal Computer and other offerings.

In order to do its work, the CPU has to know where the information it's supposed to work on is located. Therefore, it needs the address of the data, as well as the data itself. The data may be located externally such as on disk or tape. In this case the program tells the CPU where to send its read message to fetch the data. The data may already be in memory as a result of the preceding operation. In this case the CPU needs the memory address of the data. The appropriate signals are sent out on the data and address buses, and the data is fetched into the CPU registers to be worked on.

Temporary storage within the CPU is accomplished by the use of registers. They consist of flip-flops which store a bit each. Registers have special functions related to the class of information that they hold. The three classes of information that the registers hold are: data, addresses, and instructions. The registers in the CPU include: General Purpose (also known as accumulators), Memory Address (MAR), Program Counter (PC), and Instruction Register (IR). The flexibility and power of the CPU depend in part on the number and type of registers it has.

The CPU acts on the data stored in its registers. The instructions in the program tell it what to do. These functions include arithmetic operations like add, subtract, multiply, and divide; they include logical operations like comparing less than, greater than, or equal to; they include branching capabilities from one part of the program to another; and they include data movement in and out of memory, to and from peripheral devices, and within the CPU itself. The instruction set of a particular microprocessor determines what functions it can perform. The number of different instructions is one indication of the complexity or sophistication of a particular microprocessor.

The Arithmetic and Logic Unit (ALU) is comprised of special circuitry

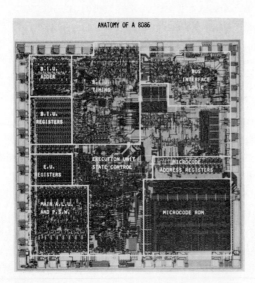

Figure 3.12 CPU functional organization, courtesy of Intel Corporation. Microphotograph.

made up of the combinational logic elements we discussed earlier. It is the place where data is actually transformed by the computer. Mathematical and logical operations on the data are performed by the ALU.

One of the great advances that occurred with the development of the microprocessor was the ability to generalize its instruction set. In the same way that Alan Turing discovered that computers could be "universal" machines by processing duplicated logic, microprocessor designers determined that the instruction set of a CPU could be generalized by implementing it in microcode. In early computers the multilevel functions of machine instructions were implemented in the hardware. Control signals were sent, memory accesses were performed, and registers were loaded by sending signals through complex hardware circuits which produced the logic necessary for each separate activity. By implementing these functions in microcode the functions of the complex circuits are replaced. The activities are broken down into subinstructions and coded in binary format. During the running of a program, a particular instruction is fetched. The microcode for it is accessed and each subinstruction is executed by the CPU. The ADD instruction, for example, is translated by the computer into a series of activities that will move the data from the CPU registers into the ALU, cause the actual addition, and store the result back into the appropriate register. When all of the substeps comprising a particular instruction have been performed, the CPU fetches the next instruction in the program. Since an instruction is now a logical entity, the way it is executed by the hardware can be changed to accommodate to the design of a particular system. Microcode usually resides in ROM (Read-Only Memory). It is not accessible to programs, but it can be changed by the manufacturer if need be. The use of microcode permits changes to hardware while minimizing the impact on software already running on machines of previous design.

Computers have crystal oscillators which act as clocks. They provide the timing so that all activities are synchronized. You can imagine what chaos would result if random signals were sent out on thousands of tiny wires without being coordinated. Certain inputs to the various logic gates are clock pulses. Output signals are thus produced on cue and are sent to the next functional area in the computer in an orderly fashion. There they become input signals waiting for the next clock pulse to become active.

CPU clock speeds are quoted in millions of pulses per second (megahertz). Early microprocessors ran in the 1-MHz range. Current speeds range from 5 to 8 MHz, and CPUs with speeds of 10 MHz and more are already in production. These speeds permit addition in a few hundred nanoseconds (billionths of a second). This is a little faster than the 0.3 sec. of Mark I.

To back up its computational tasks the CPU performs a host of control functions. These include managing the data and address buses, turning memory on and off, suspending computation to process interrupts, and a host of other housekeeping chores that coordinate the activities of the computer.

MEMORY

Memory is the work space of the computer. Although some writers include auxiliary storage media such as disk and tape under the general category of memory, we will make a distinction here. For purposes of this discussion we are talking about IC chips, magnetic bubble memories, or core memories. These are devices that are directly accessed by the CPU. No peripheral interface circuitry is required for data exchange.

MOS chips are the most commonly used type of memory in microcomputers. They are volatile. They hold data bits only so long as the power is on in the computer. Memory for earlier types of computers was made of magnetic cores which were nonvolatile. Once the core was magnetized it remained so whether or not there was electrical power in the computer. The same is true of magnetic bubbles. Once they are generated, they remain in existence and magnetized until they are erased by some form of bubble annihilator.

The major advantages of semiconductor (IC) memory are that it is fast, cool, dense, and cheap. The speed of an IC memory is determined by its access time. Average access time to read from or write to this memory is measured in nanoseconds. Today accesses fall in the 200 to 800 nsec. range.

Heat can be a problem for computers. Very large computers have water or freon cooling systems and are kept in air conditioned environments. IC chips do not require large amounts of power and do not produce a great deal of heat. Therefore, microcomputers do not require special cooling systems or heavily air conditioned environments. Various manufacturers' specifications for temperature range from 40 to 95°F. Humidity specifications range from 20 to 80 percent. In actual practice it is better to stay toward the middle of these ranges. Microcomputers really don't like to be very hot or very wet. The machines do plug into ordinary 120-V lines. If you want to be on the safe side, however, it is best to have a separate line for your computer that doesn't have anything else plugged into it.

DO YOU REALIZE, MR. WILSON, THAT YOU ARE 43 NANOSECONDS LATE?

Figure 3.13 Courtesy of Anthony Cresci.

The density of a chip refers to the number of transistors on it. We can pack a lot of transistors on a chip. Early MOS memory chips had a capacity of 1K bits. K equals 1024 which is 2^{10}. We, therefore, refer to K as roughly 1000. Memory chips in wide use today hold 64K bits of information. Soon 256K-bit chips will be the commercial norm.

Several memory chips are plugged into the board to make up the byte rating of a particular microcomputer. A 64K computer, for example, would have eight 64K-bit memory chips.

There are two main categories of memory: RAM and ROM. RAM stands for Random Access Memory. Actually it is Read/Write memory. Its cells are designed to change back and forth between 0 and 1 as dictated by the signals from the CPU. We use this kind of memory to hold our programs and data while we are working on them.

There is a kind of RAM that will hold a 0 or 1 as long as the power is on. This is called static RAM and is composed of flip-flops. Dynamic RAM, on the other hand, is composed of one transistor and a capacitor. The capacitor holds a charge for about 200 μsec. After that the charge leaks off. In order to keep the data in the cell, the charge has to be refreshed. Therefore extra circuitry is included in dynamic RAM chips to restore the charge. Even with the extra circuitry, dynamic RAM is smaller and cheaper to make than static RAM.

ROM means Read-Only Memory. In this type of memory all of the bits have been preset at the factory to their on and off states. We can't change the information on the chips by means of programs. We use this kind of memory to store instructions that don't change. Operating system instructions, language interpreters, and instructions to run other machines via a microprocessor are usually stored in ROM. Information stored in ROM is not lost when we power down a computer. This is because ROM is not made of the same types of circuits as RAM.

Although we cannot write to ROM with program instructions, some ROM can be modified. Mask-programmed ROM is loaded with its bit pattern logic during manufacture. It cannot be changed. User programmable ROM (PROM) is a special ROM that that can be changed. Each bit position is connected to the metalization pattern with a short film of metal called a fusible link. The user can use a momentary surge of electrical current to melt certain links, thereby creating a different logical output for selected cells. Of course, there is only so much modification that one can do with this type of PROM.

Erasable PROM (EPROM) can be completely reprogrammed if need be. Two methods of erasing this type of PROM are by using electricity or ultraviolet light. Erasable PROMs are much more expensive than the other types and are used mainly in the development of logic for other types of ROM.

INTERNAL ORGANIZATION

It is possible to build an entire computer on one board. For additional funtions, more than one board is often needed. The arrangements of the various chips that make up a multiboard microcomputer fall into two broad categories. Some manufacturers place their chips on two or more boards and connect the desired lines of each board with cables.

The other prevalent design uses a motherboard. A board with up to 100 lines or wires on it forms the base of the computer. A 100-line board is called an S-100 board. Chips that perform the various functions are mounted on separate boards which are then plugged into slots on the mother board perpendicular to it. The S-100 design permits easy expansion of functions. Communications may be added by plugging in a communications board, and additional memory and addi-

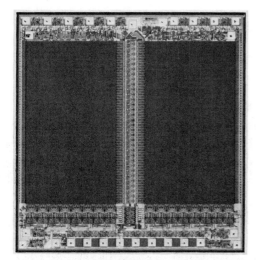

Figure 3.14 **64K-bit EPROM, courtesy of Intel** Corporation. Microphotograph.

Figure 3.15 Single-board computer, courtesy of Intel Corporation.

tional disk controllers may be added. A standard definition of the signals carried by the various lines has been adopted by the IEEE and is important so that the dip pins get connected to the right wires for sending and receiving signals. This is particularly important if boards from several manufacturers are going to be used in a S-100 machine. Many popular microcomputers permit the addition of special-function boards to a motherboard which already has chips on it that provide the basic functions of the computer. This is not an S-100 architecture, but it does give the user some of the same expansion benefits.

INPUT AND OUTPUT

Now that we have explored the internal structure and functions of the micro-computer, we turn our attention to the external universe of Input and Output (I/O) devices. In computer circles these are known as peripherals. These are pieces of hardware that permit human beings to interface with the computer. It is through the use of I/O devices that data is translated from human intentions to machine bits and then back again. Some data is stored in an intermediate form which the CPU translates and which is still incomprehensible to us. Mass storage devices such as disk and tape handle this type of data.

Humans understand numbers, letters, and other symbols. Two devices that use such symbols are Cathode Ray Tubes (CRTs) (screens) and printers. These are output devices. To get information into the computer, we commonly use some type of keyboard. The keys have the symbols we recognize on them so that we know what data we're entering. Even though it looks like the pressing of a key creates a character on the screen display, this is not what is happening in the computer. The signals are actually going to the CPU from the keyboard. They are then sent to the screen device where the hardware displays them as energized dots. Therefore, CRTs and keyboards are two different devices serving two different functions even though we often see them in the same cabinet.

There are many ways to input and output data. Since our focus is on small business computers, we will not be exploring such things as keypunching, optical character recognition, input and output generated by computers running other computers, or COM (Computer Output Microfilm).

KEYBOARDS

When a key is pressed on a keyboard, the computer interprets the signal produced by that particular key. Therefore, the depressing of a key does not directly create a character the way a typewriter does. There is a translation occurring. Because of this we can change the meaning of any key to produce any character or function we wish. An "A" on the key surface doesn't neces-

Figure 3.16 Typical microcomputer configuration, courtesy of Altos Computer Systems.

sarily have to produce an "A" in the data. In addition to standard typewriter keys, function keys are sometimes added on the sides or at the top of the keyboard. They are the ones whose functions are most often defined by the manufacturer or a program's instructions. For example, word processing functions such as insert or delete can be accomplished by depressing defined function keys. Some keyboards include numeric keypads such as those used on calculators. This design is especially useful for applications that require a lot of numeric data entry.

DISPLAYS

CRTs are the most common form of display device, although Light-Emitting Diodes (LEDs) and Liquid Crystal Displays (LCDs) are also used as microcomputer output devices. You have seen these latter types used in electronic calculators. They are a low-cost way of displaying a few characters or numbers. To have any practical value for business applications, a terminal must be capable of displaying more than eight or ten characters at a time, however. This is where CRTs come in.

The number of characters per line in standard CRT models ranges from 40 to about 100. The most common screen format is 80 characters per line. The number of lines on the screen also varies from model to model. A half-page display is about 24 lines long. A full-page display holds about 56 lines of data.

The screen may be thought of as a window on memory. The data is continuous in memory. The user can only see the amount of data the screen is capable of displaying at one time. Therefore, CRTs have scrolling capabilities. This means that the program controlling the screen will display succeeding or preceding lines of data when it recognizes the fact that a forward or reverse scroll key has been depressed on the keyboard.

The program keeps its place on the screen by means of a cursor. This is usually a rectangular symbol about the size of one character. The cursor moves automatically when letter or number keys are depressed. In order to edit previously entered data, the operator uses cursor manipulation keys to move the cursor up and down and left and right, thereby telling the computer where to recognize the entry of new information.

Screen displays are available in different color combinations to appeal to individual tastes. There are green characters on a black background, white on black, and the reverse, black on white. A new and very pleasing combination is amber on black.

The brightness of the screen can usually be adjusted. Plastic shields are also available to attach to the front of the screen. This is an important feature since glare from the screen can be very fatiguing to the user.

Screen displays or monitors are not the same as regular television sets. They are engineered for a higher quality picture and are therefore more expensive than TVs. The quality factor is called a pixel, which stands for picture element. Each pixel is a dot on the screen. The larger the number of pixels, the sharper the picture. For character presentation this is not so critical. Characters are formed by a character generator chip in the computer which determines the number and arrangement of the dots or pixels. Characters are, therefore, uniform in size and easily recognized, even if the "O" might look a little square to us. When we are using a computer for color graphics, however, the quality of the monitor becomes much more important.

The best quality color is produced by RGB monitors. Signals are sent on separate lines to each of the three color guns, red, green, and blue (hence the name, RGB) to produce the image. An alternative technology uses a composite video signal to send a rainbow of colors to the monitor on only one line.

In graphics mode the sharpness of the image is determined by the number of pixels. Low-resolution graphics uses fewer pixels which accounts for the rectangles that seem to compose a low-resolution image. High-resolution graphics uses more pixels which results in a clearer picture. The trade-off is that more memory is required to store the image, and image creation is slower.

PRINTERS

Screen devices display data temporarily. Very often, however, we wish to have a permanent record of our data. For this purpose we use printers. Microcomputer systems generally have two types of printers the user can choose between. They are dot matrix and formed character printers.

Dot matrix printers form characters from combinations of dots, usually in a 5×7 or 7×9 grid. The print head is composed of columns of pins. The computer selects the appropriate pins to strike the ribbon to form the character. Dot matrix printers are faster and cheaper than formed character printers. Common speeds are 150 to 600 lines per minute.

Dot matrix printers usually use continuous forms, that is, fan fold paper that is perforated between sheets so that the pages can be separated once the printing is completed. The paper has holes on either side of the pages which fit into a tractor-feed mechanism. The protrusions on the tractor-feed fit into the holes and pull the paper through the printer.

Formed character printers are often called letter quality printers. They use a print head which is shaped like a flat wheel ("daisy wheel") with formed characters arranged on spokes radiating from the center or as a cap (thimble) with characters arranged around the edge. An electronically controlled typewriter such as an IBM Selectric can also be adapted for use as a microcomputer printer.

These printers can print on single sheets of paper which are rolled through the platen the same way that paper is fed into a typewriter. Sheet feeder attachments are available to automatically load each individual sheet when the

This is an example of dot matrix printing.

Figure 3.17 Dot matrix characters.

printer is ready for it. Sheet feeders are very nice when many pages have to be printed, such as for large legal documents or merge letters for a long list of names.

Since the complete character strikes the ribbon in one blow, the quality of the printing is very high. The catch is that character printers are slow. Their speed is usually specified in characters per second (cps). The average range is 25 to 60 cps. This translates to approximately 25 to 60 lines per minute. At this rate, printing one full page of text can take 1 to 2 min.

Some printer manufacturers are bringing dot matrix printers to the marketplace that use a larger number of pins to form their characters than mentioned above. They also print over the same character more than once. This slows up the print speed but produces letter quality output. Such a dot matrix printer can be used at its faster speed for draft quality output and at its slower speed for correspondence-quality documents.

The speed of a printer is sometimes enhanced with bidirectional movement of the print head. One line is printed from left to right and the next line is printed from right to left as the head is returning across the page. This can be done if the printer is buffered. A buffer is a storage-area like memory which holds a certain number of lines of text to be printed. Buffering makes

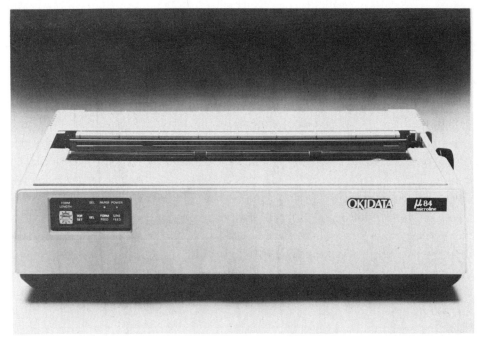

Figure 3.18 DOT matrix printer, courtesy of Okidata.

efficient use of the CPU as well. Since the internal processing speed of the microprocessor is thousands of times faster than the printer, the CPU can quickly fill up the buffer and then go on with its other work without being interrupted each time the printer wants to print the next character. When all the characters in the buffer have been printed, the next portion of the text is moved to the buffer for printing.

There are printers that do not use ribbons. They use a special roll of paper that is chemically treated. The impact of the print head on the paper forms the character as a result of the pressure or heat applied.

DISK STORAGE

Disk storage is the element that expands the computer so that it is usable for business functions. Without disk storage of some kind the microcomputer is not much more than an expensive toy. The reason is that we need enough space to accommodate our business data, and we need to be able to access this data quickly and easily.

Disks are magnetic media. They are coated with a metal oxide that has tiny iron bits impregnated in it in a random fashion. To write data on the disk, a magnetized head passes over the disk surface. The magnetic field in the head causes the iron bits to line up in one direction. A change in the polarity of the field of the head causes the bits to line up in the other direction. When the data is read from the disk, the direction of the iron bits is sensed. A change of direction tells the computer when a 1 changes to a 0 and vice versa. Therefore, the head goes along reading one or more 1s, for example, until it senses a change in polarity or direction. This tells the computer that the present character is a 0. Any number of 0s can follow until another change signals a 1 again.

Microcomputers most often use two types of disk technologies: floppy disk and Winchester-type hard disk. Floppy disks or "diskettes" are made of mylar plastic coated with metal oxide. They are soft and pliable. The two most common sizes are diameters of 5 1/4 and 8 in. Several manufacturers are beginning to introduce diskettes in smaller diameters. These are in the 3-in. range with three predominant sizes of 3, 3 1/4, and 3 1/2 in. There are also rumors of a 3.9-in. diskette. The small diskettes are called microfloppies and the 5 1/4-in. diskettes are called minifloppies. Because of engineering advances, microfloppies will hold as much data as their 5 1/4-in. cousins, or more in some cases. One version of the microfloppy comes in a rigid cartridge rather than in the more common cardboard envelope of the "flexible floppies."

The microfloppies are further evidence of the trend toward smaller and smaller components in computers. Another trend is also evident in the microfloppy case. So far there is no agreed-upon standard for size. Once more things will be confusing for a while.

Most diskettes are packaged in a cardboard holder from which they are never removed. There is a slot in the holder to permit the read/write head of the disk drive to access the surface of the diskette. The head actually touches the surface of the diskette during these operations.

The diskette is divided into tracks that are concentric circles. Each track is divided into sectors. A wedgelike area from the outer edge to the innermost track logically locates common sectors. Each track, therefore, has the same number of sectors. Figure 3.20 shows the surface of a diskette divided into tracks and sectors. The IBM 3740 standard defines the surface of an 8-in. diskette as having 77 tracks with 26 sectors per track. There are 128 bytes per sector. This adds up to 256,256 bytes on one surface of the diskette. A diskette

Figure 3.19 Diskette.

with this configuration is called single sided, single density. As you may have guessed, there is more than one way to configure a diskette. Some diskettes can be read and written on both sides. They are known as double-sided diskettes. Some manufacturers make drives and diskettes that manage twice the number of bytes in the same physical space. This is know as double density. The term "quad" disks refers to double-sided, double-density diskettes. The capacity of a single diskette can thus range from about 125,000 bytes to over 1 million bytes.

The computer recognizes the beginning of a sector by means of one or more small holes near the large center hole of the diskette. One hole means that the disk is soft sectored. The hardware senses the hole and then counts the time as the diskette revolves so that it knows where each sector of the track begins. Hard-sectored diskettes have a hole for each sector so that the computer knows where it is by sensing each perforation.

Floppy disk is a very economical storage medium. Some care must be taken in handling the diskettes, however. Since they are magnetic media, it is important to keep such things as paper clips and magnets away from them. Diskettes do eventually wear out, so the data they hold must be copied to a fresh diskette periodically. They are also limited in the amount of storage they provide.

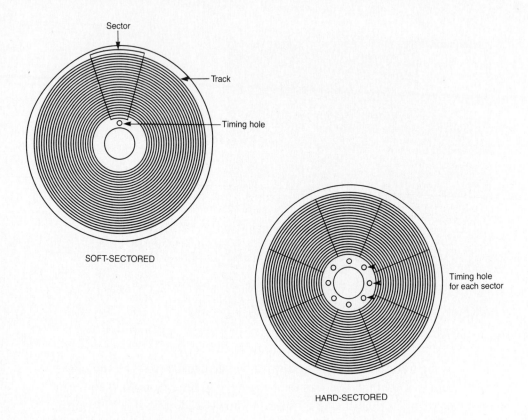

Figure 3.20 Diskette organization.

Winchester-type hard disk is, as the name implies, a rigid medium as opposed to the flexible floppy disk. It is made from a hard metal plate coated with metal oxide. The read/write head floats a few thousandths of an inch above the surface of the disk on a cushion of air created by the platter's spin. The disk is sealed in an airtight shell, and it cannot be handled by the user. The bits per inch density of this type of disk is very great. Disk diameters range from 5 1/4 to 14 in. and capacity ranges from 5 million bytes to over 100 million bytes per disk.

There is a new disk technology that holds great promise for the future. This is an optical approach that uses lasers to read and write to the disk. The laser burns a hole in the surface of the disk to indicate a binary digit. Because of the precision with which the laser beam can be controlled, the bit density of this kind of storage is enormous. A 12-in. disk can hold 2 gigabytes of data. A gigabyte is 2^{30} or approximately 1 billion bytes. The high capacity enables

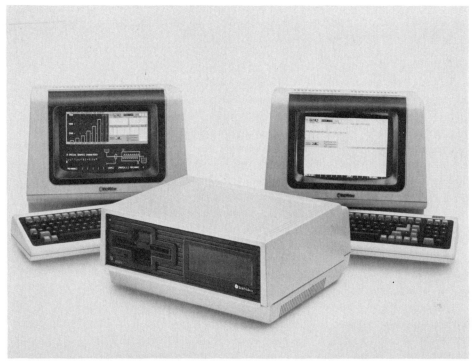

Figure 3.21 Microcomputer with Winchester-type disk, courtesy of TeleVideo Systems, Inc.

the use of optical disk for the storage of voice, picture, and data on one medium. The major disadvantage of this technology so far is that it is not erasable. Once the hole is made it is a permanent record. Research is continuing, however, and optical disk may become a very important storage medium in the future.

TAPES

Magnetic tape is not used widely for microcomputer business applications. There are several reasons why. It is all right for backup purposes if you want to make a copy of an entire disk in case something happens to the original. Then you can copy the data to a new disk if need be. This is not too important a function for floppy disk since you can always copy the information onto another diskette. In the early days before diskettes, tape cassettes were used to store programs and data for microcomputers. The programs and data were loaded into memory to be processed by the computer. This scheme was adequate for processing small amounts of information. The amount of memory limited the size of programs and the amount of data that could be processed conveniently.

Since tape is a sequential medium you have to start at the beginning and read through the reel until you come to the record you need. Disk is much more convenient to use because the head can be positioned on any track and sector to access the required information.

There is a type of tape that is becoming quite important. This is called streaming tape. It is used to back up hard disks. Since hard disks hold so much data, it is inconvenient to use a lot of diskettes to store the backup. Streaming tapes hold millions of bytes, so using them for backup is much more efficient. The tape moves very fast as the bits are transferred to it. Several million bits can be transferred in 1 sec. An entire disk can be copied in a matter of a few minutes. To restore the disk, the data is copied back from the tape in the same kind of stream. This type of tape is not used to copy individual records which is a much slower process and which requires stopping for inter-record gaps (blank spaces on the tape between records).

PERIPHERAL INTERFACES

A peripheral interface connects the CPU and memory to the peripherals attached to the computer. A peripheral interface can be a single IC chip or an entire circuit board, depending on how complex the functions are that it is required to perform. Its job is to direct the input and output traffic of the computer as data moves to and from the various peripherals. It performs translation of the various data forms so that the CPU can understand the input and the selected device can accept the output.

There are two common physical types of paths for sending and receiving data between the CPU and its peripherals: parallel and serial transmission. Parallel transmission means that 8 data bits are sent over a set of wires in unison. Serial transmission means that 1 bit is sent after another over one wire.

Serial bits may be sent in a regular pulse or beat, sort of like using a metronome. That means the peripheral interface and the receiving device have gotten synchronized with each other. The pulses are counted and accumulated into characters. When the CPU has no data to send, the devices send synchronizing characters to keep their timing right.

Another method of sending serial transmissions is asynchronously. The beginning and end of each character (byte) are marked by start and stop bits. This way the data can arrive at any time since each character is delineated. The receiving device counts the bits to recognize each character as it arrives.

There is a voltage standard for serial transmission called RS232. This specifies what voltage is required to define a 0 or 1 so that the device can distinguish data from noise on the line. Peripheral devices are often advertised as being RS232 compatible.

Serial transmission is simpler, slower and usually cheaper than parallel transmission. It is usually used when a peripheral is located at some distance from the CPU since cables for parallel transmission are very expensive.

Devices that use parallel transmission are typically high-speed peripherals such as disk and tape drives. CRTs, keyboards, and printers can use either. Therefore, when a system is selected and configured, it is necessary to know the specifications for the peripherals that are going to be used.

COMMUNICATIONS

Small business needs generally will not require communications capabilities. It is useful to know a little about communications, however, in case the need should arise. Communications means that a terminal, or even another computer, is sending and receiving data to and from a computer to which it is not directly wired. For example, if your business had a computer in the main office and a CRT in the warehouse, you would probably use communications to send and receive information.

There are several things to consider about communications. They include the form of the data that is being sent (the bit patterns), the speed at which the bits are moving (the baud rate or transfer rate), and the types of wires and equipment used to transmit the data.

The most common medium for communications is telephone company lines. Most often, telephone lines work in analog mode. This means that the signal is a series of waves. Business computers work in digital mode. In order to translate the digital signals to analog waves at the sending end and then back again to digital signals at the receiving end, we use modems. Modem stands for modulate-demodulate. We use a pair of modems, one at the sending end and a matching one at the receiving end, to accomplish the necessary signal changes.

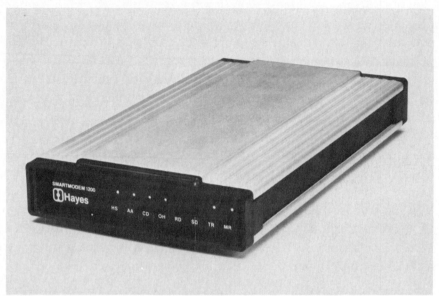

Figure 3.22 External modem, courtesy of Hayes Microcomputer Products, Inc.

Figure 3.23 Internal modem board, courtesy of Hayes Microcomputer Products, Inc.

The telephone company also offers digital transmission service which does not require that the signal be converted between analog and digital forms. A different kind of line interface device is used in this case.

Lines can operate in one direction only or they operate in both directions (send and receive). A one-way communication is called simplex. If the line can be turned around but only operates in one direction at a time, it is called half-duplex. A line that operates in both directions simultaneously is called full-duplex. Modems vary according to the type of transmission selected. The factors that determine selection are speed, response time, the amount and direction of data to be communicated, and, of course, cost.

A user can use already installed telephone lines to dial up the computer he wants to communicate with. This method requires that the signal go through the telephone switching network. The line is susceptible to the traffic and noise associated with such usage since voice communications are also going on. An alternative option is to install a dedicated or "leased" line which connects the terminal directly to the computer. This is a more reliable, and also a more expensive, solution.

The computer has to understand the message that it is receiving. To do this a series of control characters is used. The meanings of the characters and their placement in the message is called a protocol. The communication protocol defines the meanings of the special characters that are sent as part of a message to indicate where it begins and ends, how long it is, and other such information. The most common protocol is the "teletype" (TTY) format, the bit pattern that was used in teletype transmissions long before computers started communicating. Another protocol that defines the control characters in a different manner from TTY protocol is ASCII. We have already discussed the ASCII character set. IBM 3270 is another format. It is more frequently used when communicating with a large mainframe computer.

The speed is a function of how many bits are sent over the line per second. 300 baud means 300 bits per second are being transmitted. Common speeds for serial transmissions range between 300 and 9600 baud. These are the speeds that are commonly supported by the telephone company.

There are other communications paths besides telephone company lines, such as satellite or microwave transmissions. They are expensive and are used by large companies that have massive amounts of data to transmit.

The lack of standardization among computers poses a problem for information interchange. It is generally not possible to hook one manufacturer's computer directly to another manufacturer's computer and have the two understand each other. Standard protocols like the teletype or 3270 formats, however, do permit the exchange of information using communications regardless of the internal format of any particular computer.

Local Area Networks

There are alternatives to connecting peripheral devices to computers or computers to computers by means of modems. In an office environment a business may have the need for more than one work station for inputting data. The solution may be to acquire several microcomputers and connect them together so that they can all access the same files. If the computers are going to be used only for applications like VisiCalc then access to common files might not be required. Connecting things together is important when several workers have to use common data such as the customer file or the product file. The connections under discussion can be accomplished by use of Local Area Networks (LANs). A cable is used to connect all of the devices together. Special chips are installed in each micro to control access to the cable. They determine whether or not the cable is busy, that is, whether or not some other device is using it. When the cable is free, the requesting device sends its message to another device on the line. The recipient may be another micro or it may be a file server, that is, a large disk drive with a controlling chip that holds the central files that the stations wish to access.

This type of connection is called baseband. It is used for data transmissions only. One advantage is in providing hardware redundancy so that similar machines are available if one fails. Critical jobs can always be done by shifting the workload. Each processor runs its own programs rather than having one CPU service the needs of several terminals as is the case with a typical multiuser system.

Private Branch Exchange (PBX)

The PBX is another alternative for connecting terminals and computers within an office. In this scheme a private telephone switching device is installed in the office. It services both voice and data. This means that all the phones are hooked up to it as well as the computers. The PBX is connected to the telephone network so that an external link is provided to the outside world. Modems can be attached to the PBX to establish communications with off-site locations.

SPEECH SYNTHESIS

Approximations of the human voice can be output from a computer, in other words, the computer can be made to talk. The "words" are stored as bit patterns on disk the same way that graphics images are stored, and they are located in digital files. When the computer program wants to say something, it selects the desired words and sends them to a piece of hardware that converts the digital signals to analog signals and sends them out through a speaker. If numbers have been stored in the computer, then an on-line bill paying program, for example, could be coded to tell the customer the amount that it had just received by a touch-tone phone in payment.

The quality of the sound output by computers is not very satisfying at the moment, but the capability for computers to talk certainly exists.

VOICE RECOGNITION

Talking to the computer is another matter entirely. One thing that is relatively easy to do is to input words or messages into a computer. A programmer can speak into a microphone, and the computer can digitize the signals and create a binary file. If different files are created, and the programmer knows what each one contains, then the appropriate one can be selected to convey a message to a user depending on what the program wants to output.

On the other hand, getting the computer to recognize the same word spoken by many different people is extremely difficult. The spoken command can be input and digitized as we mentioned above. It can then be compared to data already stored in the computer. The catch is that voice characteristics are as varied as fingerprints. If a person has a cold, the current digitized pattern will be different from the voice pattern without a cold. Under these circumstances, the computer won't recognize what the person is saying. We are going to have to wait a while longer before we can call up our friendly neighborhood computer and order our groceries.

4

Software

We have studied the hardware of a computer, the CPU, memory, and peripherals. We know about the physical organization and operation of the machine. If this was all there was to a computer, the machine would not be of any use to anyone. We need logical capabilities to convert the hardware into a useful, functioning tool. These logical capabilities come to us by means of software. The major logical capabilities we need are:

1. Logic to direct the operations of the CPU, peripherals and memory (an operating system and other system software),
2. Logic that converts human instructions to machine instructions (assemblers, compilers, interpreters),
3. Logic that manipulates data (application programs).

OPERATING SYSTEMS

The operating system is a set of programs that controls the functions of the computer. One of its functions is initializing the system. This requires verifying what peripherals are attached to the system and knowing what signals are required to send data to them or to accept data from them. Operating systems often have code that will do a diagnostic check on the system when it is first turned on to be sure everything is running in order. On large computers the operating system can reconfigure the hardware around some malfunctioning unit, such as a faulty disk drive, so that the computer can be used without the faulty part. Once the system is initialized, it is ready to process data.

There are different operating systems for different microcomputers depending on which CPU chip the manufacturer has selected for the machine. Apple and Radio Shack computers have proprietary operating systems. One well-known operating system is called CP/M$^{®}$ which stands for Control Program for Microcomputers. It was developed by Digital Research of Pacific Grove, California, and it will run on any computer using Intel 8080 or Zilog Z80 CPU chips. MP/M is the multiuser version, and CP/M-86 is the 16-bit version. There is a large body of application software on the marketplace which runs on computers that have a CP/M operating system.

Another operating system for microcomputers is MS-DOS which is licensed by Microsoft. It runs on several machines including the IBM Personal Computer.

When we wish to process data, the operating system manages things so that the various units of the computer work in the proper order. If we wish to run an accounting application, for example, we have to load the accounting programs into the computer. The operating system must recognize the command that we key in on the keyboard and identify the program we want to run. When we enter commands of this kind we are communicating directly with the operating system. The operating system must then find the beginning of the program on the disk and read some of the code into memory. It must do a host of housekeeping chores to allocate memory space for our data, to locate any files that our program uses, and to accept input from us for the program to work on. It must also manage the proper outputting of data from the program by writing to disk files or sending information to the printer or whatever else is required.

The operating system locates programs and data files by keeping a directory of the information on each disk. The first thing that must be done to a blank disk is to initialize it. This function formats the disk so that a directory can be created to store information about files.

CP/M sets up a File Control Block (FCB) in the directory for a file when the file is first created. The FCB stores the name of the file. As records are written to the file, their addresses are stored in the FCB. Since the location of the records is known, the individual records do not have to be in physically sequential locations but can be placed in any unused spaces on the disk. A disk file can thus be read randomly because the operating system knows the address of the particular record the program is seeking.

Another function that the operating system performs is managing foreground and background processing. We may be entering our data in one section of the program while some other activity, such as printing, is going on in another part of the program. This is a form of multitasking. Systems that can manage foreground and background activities are more complex than those that only do one thing at a time.

Some operating systems have the ability to store information that is to be printed in a disk file in printer format. The information is printed out at a later time. This is called spooling and is very useful in permitting a program to finish its work if the printer is tied up on another job.

A very important function of the operating system is to manage incoming and outgoing messages. This requires linking the terminal to the program so that the data is processed appropriately. If there are several users on the system, each one has to have his messages processed by the specific logic applicable to his activity. We don't want to be doing general ledger functions in the order entry program, and we don't want to be updating the product file with customer information.

If we have a multiuser system, the operating system performs its functions for each user on the system and manages the sharing of the memory and disk in an orderly fashion. You can see that managing one user is complicated enough. Multiuser operating systems (also called multitasking systems or multiprogramming systems) are much more complex than single-user operating systems.

Other operating systems for microcomputers which manage multitasking environments are UNIX, OASIS, and the UCSD (University of California at San Diego) P-system.

PROGRAMMING LANGUAGES

We have been discussing the management of the hardware by the operating system. The operating system is software. It was written for the computer by programmers using a computer language. The programs that manipulate data are also written in programming languages. Operating systems are much more complex than applications so writing them requires a higher level of programming expertise. Systems programmers are among the highest paid group in the programming fellowship.

As we discussed in the previous chapter, the logic of computer circuits is implemented through the use of transistors that store and pass 0s and 1s. In the early days of computers the 0s and 1s were loaded directly into the computer. Programming was accomplished at the machine level in binary machine language. It was quite a job to discover errors in these endless binary strings. So computer languages were developed to make the awful task of programming more comprehensible. The first level of sophistication was the development of mnemonics for the machine language instructions or "op codes" (operation codes). This was a one-for-one equivalence of assembler mnemonic for binary instruction. A program called an assembler translated the mnemonics into machine language. While the same number of instructions still had to be coded, the form was much friendlier. Additionally, some logic could be built into the assembler to recognize syntax errors.

All programming languages have a syntax that must be followed in order to create code that the computer can execute. If you wish to add, the syntax requires that you specify the things that you wish to add together. If you leave out the operands, the computer can't perform the operation. Checking for operands is something the computer can do.

We cannot assume that getting the syntax correct is all there is to it, however. There may be logic flaws in the program that will give erroneous results. For example, if we want to calculate net profit, and we add the tax to the gross profit instead of subtracting it, the program will go merrily on its way executing a perfectly legal instruction. We won't be quite so happy obtaining the wrong amount. On the other hand, if we try to add two names together, we'll get a syntax error because the add instruction cannot operate on data that we have defined to be alphabetic.

In assembler language adding is not simply a matter of defining data variables and saying ADD. We have to move the data into the right CPU registers or specify the memory location of the data for the CPU before we can perform the operation. After we do add, we have to specify the destination of the results, either in a register or in a memory location. Working in assembler is a detailed, laborious process. It requires the coding of a great number of instructions.

A disassembler is a program that converts object or machine code back

ASSEMBLER LANGUAGE

Assembler language uses mnemonics for instructions. DCR, for example, means decrement, or subtract one. MOV means move the contents of one register into the other register. Both registers are named as operands. Operands include CPU registers, such as A or B, numbers such as 08, or memory locations such as hexadecimal 010D.

Label	Instructions	Operands
START	MVI	B,08
	MVI	C,00
	LXI	H,0119
	MOV	A,M
	CMP	C
	JC	010D
	MOV	C,A
	INX	H
	DCR	B
	JNZ	0107

Figure 4.1. A sample of assembler instructions.

to assembler language mnemonics. This function can be very helpful if the original listing of the assembler language program gets lost.

To make programming easier, other programming languages were developed that permitted the programmer to use instructions that were composites of several machine language instructions. A program called a compiler checked the syntax and converted the high-level instructions into machine language. Programmers were moving farther away from the machine. Two early "high-level" languages that are still widely used are COBOL (Common Business Oriented Language) and FORTRAN (Formula Translation). The first is used in business applications. It has an English-like syntax that permits the programmer to say things like "ADD SALARY TO OVER-TIME-PAY GIVING GROSS-PAY." You can see that the language is easy to use and that it is also self-documenting. If the programmer chooses descriptive data names such as GROSS-PAY, it's pretty easy for another programmer to understand what the instruction is all about if he has to make changes.

FORTRAN is very good for scientific and mathematical programs since its syntax supports the use of formulas very easily. It is not as good for manipulating alphabetic data as COBOL is.

The most popular language for microcomputers is BASIC (Beginners' All-Purpose Symbolic Instruction Code). As the name implies, it is a simple language for beginners to learn and use. It lacks some of the power and flexibility of other languages, but it is more than adequate for most business applications. Most of the packaged software available today for microcomputers is written in BASIC.

The way that BASIC programs are translated by the computer is a little different from the way COBOL programs are handled. The computer uses an interpreter rather than a compiler to translate the instructions into machine language. As each BASIC instruction is executed during the running of the program, it is checked and converted to machine code. If there is a syntax error, a message is displayed at the error point and the program is aborted. If a program is to be run many times, this scheme is somewhat inefficient. Compilers, on the other hand, produce object code, which is machine language, for the entire program. They also indicate errors at the time that compilation takes place. Therefore, a program with errors must be "debugged" and the errors corrected.

Once the program is "clean," the object code can be executed as many times as the user desires without further translation. Compilers do exist for BASIC, in addition to interpreters, so that once a BASIC program is created

"IN THE FUTURE, HARGREAVES, WE WOULD PREFER IT IF YOU WOULD USE MORE RIGOROUS MEANS THAN TAROT CARDS TO DEBUG PROGRAMS."

Figure 4.2 Courtesy of Fred Jackson.

and debugged using an interpreter, it can be compiled to produce object code for repetitive use.

Another language that is popular for use on microcomputers is PASCAL. PASCAL is a structured language that supports the use of subroutines at successively dependent levels. It is more complex than BASIC and gives the programmer more flexibility and more powerful instructions to work with.

BASIC* Code

```
20    INPUT "ENTER BEGINNING NUMBER"; B
30    INPUT "ENTER ENDING NUMBER"; E
50    FOR X = B TO E STEP 1
60    PRINT "NUMBER"; X
70    NEXT X
80    PRINT "DO YOU WISH TO CONTINUE? ENTER Y OR N"
90    INPUT C$
100   IF C$ = "N" GOTO 120
110   GOTO 20
120   PRINT "THANK YOU. I'M TIRED."
130   END
```

This is a fragment of code that might be used in a BASIC program. It illustrates a looping technique. It asks the user to enter a beginning and an ending number to determine the range of the loop. The messages shown in quotation marks in lines 20 and 30 are displayed on the screen so that the user knows what to enter. First he enters a beginning number which is stored in variable B. Then he enters an ending number which is stored in variable E. Line 50 establishes the loop. It sets variable X equal to the beginning number. It specifies the ending number as the value stored in E. It adds 1 to X each time line 50 is executed (STEP 1). There is only one instruction inside the loop. It displays the current value of X on the screen (line 60). PRINT in the BASIC language means "display on the screen." Line 70, NEXT X, returns the program to line 50 where 1 is added to X again. When the value of X equals the value of E, the loop is ended, and the program goes to line 80. A message is displayed asking the user if he wishes to continue. Line 90 accepts the answer. Line 100 tests to see if the user entered an "N." If he did, the program branches to line 120 (GOTO 120). If he entered anything else, line 110 directs the program back to line 20, and the process begins again.

*Beginners' All-Purpose Symbolic Instruction Code

Figure 4.3. A sample of BASIC code.

Procedural and Nonprocedural Languages

All of the languages that we have discussed so far are *procedural* languages. The logic flows step by step to create a procedure for solving a particular problem and producing a particular result. Accounting systems, for example, flow logically from the input of transactions through the calculations necessary to produce the total figures required by the business. Programs to produce these results are written in procedural languages. It requires a degree of programming skill to write such programs.

Microcomputers are in very wide use, and not all users are programmers. Therefore, software to let nontechnical users make productive use of the computer is very desirable.

Nonprocedural languages permit users to access data and accomplish selected tasks by entering certain predefined instructions. Users don't have to write entire programs to satisfy their needs.

Nonprocedural tools include data base query languages that let managers extract information from a data base, screen formatters that let users design formats for CRTs, and report generators that let the user describe the layout and fields for printed reports. Of course, the logic that makes these nonprocedural tools work is written in procedural languages.

"THIS PROGRAM USES SIX COMMANDS:
FIND, ADD, CHANGE, VIDEO, PRINT- AND IF
YOU FLUB - RIDICULE"

Figure 4.4 Courtesy of Sandy Dean.

COMMUNICATIONS

In addition to hardware which connects CPUs and peripherals for communications, software is required. Data must be taken from application programs and formatted into the messages that are to be sent. The sending and receiving of the characters in the messages must be managed. Messages must be reformatted since they are received from communicating devices and delivered to application programs expecting them. These functions are performed by special programs written to handle communications.

APPLICATION SOFTWARE

Application software is what the user is most directly concerned with. It consists of the programs that actually manipulate our data. Such programs are most often written in high-level languages and are increasingly being developed and sold as end products. Very often only the object code is available so the buyer cannot modify the package he has bought. If the source code is available, it generally costs some more than object code versions of the programs. In this case the buyer will know all the secrets of the program and can "borrow" ideas for resale. Software houses are prey to theft and plagiarism since copyright infringement is very difficult to police.

Application software may be classed as horizontal or vertical. Horizontal software crosses industry boundaries. Examples of this class are accounting packages, personnel and human resources programs, word processing software, and data base managers. Vertical software is industry specific. This type includes packages for insurance, banking and finance, education, and professional offices. Software vendors may offer software in both classes. Usually, though, a vendor picks one field or approach and develops a high level of expertise in it.

As we discussed in Chapter 1, the type of software depends on the information needs of the user. Some major categories of software are:

1. Software that is used in business or professions.
2. Office automation software.
3. Software that provides generalized functions and utilities.

Business and Professional Software

Accounting Software.   Software vendors generally market a package of accounting software consisting of the common modules that are needed to manage the books of a business. The modules include Order Entry, Accounts Receivable, Accounts Payable, Payroll, and General Ledger. Recurring data, such as sales information, is usually captured at the front end of the system in the Order Entry module and is passed on to the succeeding modules without the need to reenter it.

The utility of the package is enhanced if the programs are "user friendly," that is, if the programs are easy to use. Some techniques for "humanizing" packages include guiding the user in his activities by means of menus (lists of various activities to choose from) and by providing a "HELP" function that gives explanations about various activities on the CRT. The documentation that comes with the package is crucial. The programs may be very powerful and sophisticated, but if you can't find out how to do something, that function does not exist for you.

A sample of an accounts receivable menu might include the following functions:

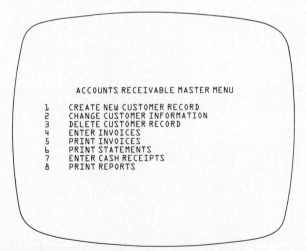

```
        ACCOUNTS RECEIVABLE MASTER MENU

    1    CREATE NEW CUSTOMER RECORD
    2    CHANGE CUSTOMER INFORMATION
    3    DELETE CUSTOMER RECORD
    4    ENTER INVOICES
    5    PRINT INVOICES
    6    PRINT STATEMENTS
    7    ENTER CASH RECEIPTS
    8    PRINT REPORTS
```

Figure 4.5 Accounts receivable master menu.

If the user selected #8 PRINT REPORTS, a second menu would be displayed, asking him to select the report(s) he wanted.

    If the user selected #1 CREATE NEW CUSTOMER RECORD, the next screen he would see might look something like:

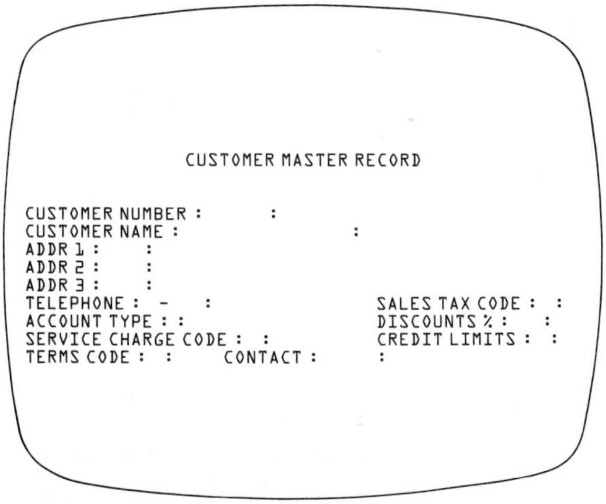

```
                    CUSTOMER MASTER RECORD

CUSTOMER NUMBER :        :
CUSTOMER NAME :                    :
ADDR 1 :      :
ADDR 2 :      :
ADDR 3 :      :
TELEPHONE :  -    :            SALES TAX CODE :  :  :
ACCOUNT TYPE :  :              DISCOUNTS % :     :
SERVICE CHARGE CODE :  :       CREDIT LIMITS :  :
TERMS CODE :  :     CONTACT :        :
```

Figure 4.6 Customer master record.

At this point the data entry operator would key in the information in the bracketed spaces, thereby creating a new customer record. All orders that this new customer placed would then be linked to this information by the program to create the appropriate information for invoicing and for the General Ledger. In the example of the master menu we have shown the choice of entering invoices. This could conceivably be for changes, since most Accounts Receivable packages will automatically create invoices from orders if the orders are specified as complete to the system.

    Established software houses usually support their software. If bugs are discovered, the vendor fixes them and sends "patches" to registered buyers. Additionally, as enhancements are made to the programs, they are available to purchasers as upgrades. Since needs are always changing, software is always changing too. It is a mistake to think that once you buy a package, you're all done. Packages are generalized for a class of users. That's the way the vendor finds a large enough market to make the product profitable. This means the user will rarely have an exact match to his specific needs. Up to a point, a certain amount of customization can be done to packaged software. Some companies hire programmers to add to or change certain aspects of the programs they buy. The catch here is that the vendor may not support the package if it is changed.

Manufacturing Software.   This type of software is concerned with the data needs of manufacturing companies. It includes production scheduling, materials management, Bill of Materials handling (the hierarchical ordering of the components and their subassemblies as they are used to make a product), the tracking of work in process as it moves from one work station to the next, and the accounting for finished goods.

In addition to the above information, CAD/CAM hardware and software is available for manufacturing. CAD stands for Computer-Aided Design and CAM for Computer-Aided Manufacturing. The design of new machines such as automobiles or airplanes can be accomplished with software tools that use graphics and engineering programs.

Once the machine is designed on the computer, it can be manufactured according to the specifications that were developed during the design phase. Robots and other computers can be used to aid in the manufacturing process.

Generally CAD/CAM is used by large companies who run the software on large computers since the software is very complex and also quite expensive.

Retail Software.   This type of software, called POS (Point of Sale), manages a retail sales environment. It records sales, updates inventory, and provides links to accounting software for customer billing purposes. It captures transactions as they happen, thereby providing management with the latest information about inventory status. Many large department stores have POS systems with one or more terminals in each department attached to a central computer. Small systems, including single-user cash register computers, are available for the small entrepreneur.

Professional Software.   The needs of professionals such as doctors and lawyers are a little different from those of the business person. The major difference is that professionals are selling time or services while business people are selling goods. Therefore, an accounts receivable package for a business does not usually meet the needs of a professional. A professional billing package handles the special needs of the professional practitioner. Packages are most commonly available for the medical, dental, legal, and accounting professions.

Other.   There is software to meet the needs of many other specialized groups. However, you will not find as many off-the-shelf offerings in these areas as in the ones we have already discussed. Some members of this group include human resources, banking and finance, energy, education, real estate, and travel.

If you are looking for specialized software, the best thing to do is to seek out a company in your field that is already computerized and see if it is happy with its system. If so find out what it is and where to get it. It is best not to buy the first of something unless you are long on patience and love technical challenges.

It is important to realize that the type of business creates the information needs, and that packaged software is not necessarily transportable from one discipline to another. In the discussion of general utility software that follows the Office Automation section, you will see how it is sometimes possible to create custom-tailored programs for particular needs.

OFFICE AUTOMATION

Office automation is one of the most rapidly expanding areas in the computer field today. Offices of all sizes are automating more and more of their functions as efficient, labor-saving hardware and software products become available in the marketplace.

Word Processing

There is a fundamental difference between word processing and data processing. Word processing is concerned with the manipulation of text, that is, strings of characters that are separated by spaces. Data processing, on the other hand, is concerned with the manipulation of fields or elements of data that have specific meaning. Last name, for example, is an element with meaning in the context of a program. It can be sorted in alphabetical order, and it can be used as a key to locate other information about the person the field represents. A letter or a memo is an undifferentiated collection of characters and spaces. This is not to say that the computer does not perform operations on text, but such activities are very different from those performed on data.

Text manipulation involves entering text into the computer initially and then editing it once it's captured. Some of the editing capabilities of word processors include inserting additional text within a word or line, replacing, deleting, moving, or copying text. Text refers to anything from one character to many pages. Special functions include the ability to search for a string of one or more characters and to replace one or more of its occurrences with another string.

Formatting operations can be performed on text. Word processors permit the setting and changing of margins, the alignment of the right margin on the page (right justification), the inclusion of automatic headings and footings on each page, the automatic specification and alignment of columns, word hyphenation, and the ability to change the pitch or character size to be used for the printed document (depending on the kind of printer used).

Pagination is a very important feature of word processors. Once the top and bottom margins and the number of lines on the page have been defined, the word processing software will automatically start a new page when the current one is filled. If the user wishes to change the page format, the word processor will automatically rearrange the text and renumber the pages. Some word processors have capabilities for eliminating widows and orphans, that is, the first line of a paragraph at the end of a page or the last line of a paragraph at the beginning of a page.

Some word processors permit limited mathematical operations on columns of figures within the text. Strictly speaking, this is data processing, not word processing.

A word processor is a great deal more than a typewriter look-alike. This is due to the fact that the text is constantly moving. If information is inserted, moved, or deleted, all following text on the page is rearranged. The insertion of a large amount of text can cause a page to overrun its physical limitations. Repagination is then required to rearrange all of the following pages.

Beginning operators are sometimes put off by the fluid nature of the text they are dealing with. Once an operator is hooked, however, he or she never wants to use a typewriter again. Because it is possible to "erase" mistakes and typographical errors so easily, operators find that they can type very fast using word processors. A further benefit is that the text is entered once via the keyboard and stored on disk. It can then be recalled at any time for modification or printing. The entire document never has to be keyed more than once.

Data files can be merged with word processing documents to produce customized letters. The same text is repeated for each name on the list, and an original copy of the letter is thus created for each entry. A matching envelope can also be produced from the same list. Some word processors also permit the inclusion of data fields such as "amount due" in a dunning letter, for example. Data can either be entered by an operator during the printing of the letter, or it can be stored in the file as the name and address are so that printing is uninterrupted.

Word processors can also be used to edit source code files for programs written in high-level languages. Most operating systems have editors for source code manipulation, but they do not have the same degree of text manipulation flexibility that word processors have.

Electronic Mail

Word processing is not the only function that goes on in an office. More and more vendors are offering electronic tools to overcome some of the major inefficiencies in offices. Electronic mail is a communication service that permits users connected to a system to send messages to each other's terminals. The receiver has an electronic "in-box." When he logs on to the system, he can receive any waiting messages. The computer can notify the sender if and when a message was received. This is one way to solve the "telephone tag" problem that is so prevalent in offices today. It's pretty hard for the receiver to claim that he didn't get the message, too.

Document Storage and Retrieval

Another office automation tool is document storage and retrieval. Some word processors are stand-alone, single-user systems. Documents on these systems are available to the user by looking up their titles on the disk index. For multi-user systems, however, all documents can be stored in a central disk file and can be retrieved by any user on the system with a valid password. Key word search capabilities are available which can retreive all documents containing a certain word or sequence of words entered by the user. This eliminates those frantic searches for that memo that was written "about three weeks ago, you think, to Joe Jones, about the new product, #1245." All you have to do is ask for all documents with #1245 in them and the system will retrieve them for you.

Calendar Management

Calendar management is another very useful tool. Users of the system enter their appointment schedule into the computer. When a special meeting has to be arranged, each participant's calendar can be checked to see about his availability. Some mutually convenient time can then be arranged for all concerned parties. Calendars can be checked to avoid missing appointments, also.

GENERAL UTILITY SOFTWARE

General utilities are defined here as certain classes of software packages that are available on the marketplace that permit the user to create his own customized environment. They are tools that apply a general set of programmed commands to the user's data thereby structuring it so that he can use the computer to manipulate it. The packages permit the user to interact with the computer in nonprocedural ways so that he does not have to buy off-the-shelf applications or create custom coded programs. The two most widely used general utilities are data base managers and electronic spreadsheets.

Data Base Managers

Data base managers are programs that permit the user to enter commands and select options from menus to create a data base. The user tells the program the name of the data element and its characteristics, whether it is numeric or alphabetic, how many characters it contains, what its minimum and maximum values can be, and other defining characteristics. Once the fields in the data base are defined, actual data can be entered and stored for subsequent processing.

Instead of using application programs which supply predefined screen formats (such as the Customer Master Record in our previous example), the user can create his own formats and set up records according to his needs. Perhaps the business needs "Bill To" and "Ship To" names and addresses or wants to see year-to-date sales figures in the customer record. If he can't find a package that keeps this information, the user can create it with a data base manager.

Functions that are commonly available include four-function math which permits adding, subtracting, multiplying, and dividing of numeric fields, adding, deleting, sorting, and merging of alphabetic data, and report generation. Sometimes a report generator is used in conjunction with the data in the data base if a large number of reports in different formats is required.

Once the data base is created, it can be accessed by custom programs coded in procedural languages such as BASIC, or it can be used to provide input to word processing systems.

One of the most desirable capabilities of a data base management system is the ability to inquire into the data base and to produce ad hoc reports by entering some simple commands. Records can be sorted and selected based on the entered parameters. For example, the user can instruct the data base manager to find all accounts with a balance due for which no payment has been made in the last month.

Given this kind of flexibility, a great deal can be done with data base managers. If your processing needs can be met within the capabilities of a data base manger, then you don't need application software to do the job. This is not always the case, however. Data manipulation requirements for handling business data are usually complex enough to require application software to fulfill them. Data base managers provide a convenient way of establishing data bases to be used by applications, and they are very good for structuring and storing data to be used for purposes such as management information and report generation.

Electronic Spreadsheets

This type of utility is one of the most useful computer tools to appear on the marketplace. Products such as VisiCalc and SuperCalc have greatly eased the forecasting and modeling burdens of business planners and managers. An electronic spreadsheet permits the user to enter his data into a two-dimensional grid of rows and columns. Since the grid or worksheet is larger than the display area of the user's CRT, only part of the data is visible to the user at a given time. He can, however, scroll through the data, accessing any column and row in the worksheet that he desires.

The user defines the relationship of the data in one cell to that of data

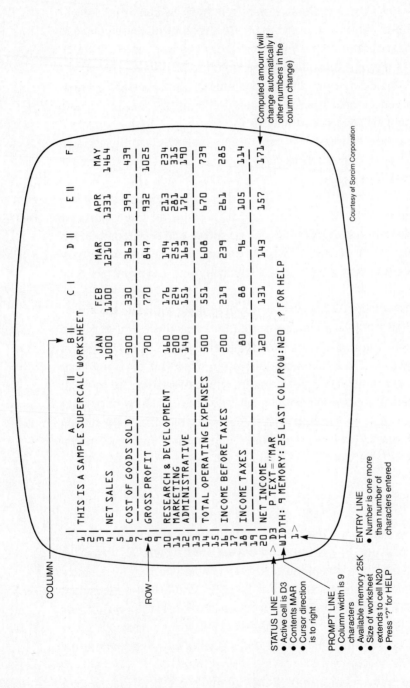

COLUMN

ROW

	A	B ||	C		D ||	E ||	F	
1	THIS IS A SAMPLE SUPERCALC WORKSHEET						
2		JAN	FEB	MAR	APR	MAY	
3	NET SALES	1000	1100	1210	1331	1464	
4							
5	COST OF GOODS SOLD	300	330	363	399	439	
6							
7	GROSS PROFIT	700	770	847	932	1025	
8							
9							
10	RESEARCH & DEVELOPMENT	160	176	194	213	234	
11	MARKETING	200	224	251	281	315	
12	ADMINISTRATIVE	140	151	163	176	190	
13							
14	TOTAL OPERATING EXPENSES	500	551	608	670	739	
15							
16	INCOME BEFORE TAXES	200	219	239	261	285	
17							
18	INCOME TAXES	80	88	96	105	114	
19							
20	NET INCOME	120	131	143	157	171	

> D3   P TEXT="MAR
WIDTH: 9 MEMORY: 25 LAST COL/ROW:N20   ? FOR HELP

1 >

Computed amount (will change automatically if other numbers in the column change)

STATUS LINE
• Active cell is D3
• Contents MAR
• Cursor direction is to right

PROMPT LINE
• Column width is 9 characters
• Available memory 25K
• Size of worksheet extends to cell N20
• Press "?" for HELP

ENTRY LINE
• Number is one more than number of characters entered

Courtesy of Sorcim Corporation

Figure 4.7 A typical SuperCalc screen, courtesy of Sorcim Corporation.

in another cell. He can tell the program to take a certain amount, increase it by 20 percent and add the result to each of the next 15 rows or columns. He can perform various mathematical functions on combinations of cells. He can change the data in the cells and recalculate the results. Activities that used to take hours or even days with a calculator can now be accomplished in minutes on the computer.

Print commands are included to provide the user with hard-copy reports if needed.

GRAPHICS

Graphics capabilities are really a combination of hardware and software functions. As we mentioned in the screen display section, graphics color monitors are used to display graphics images. These images can be created in several different ways.

Business graphics are usually produced by a business graphics software program. Charts and graphs are created using business data in the computer's files. Output is available on a CRT or in hard-copy from a printer or plotter.

Creating forms and pictures on a computer is a much more complicated affair. A graphics tablet may be used to draw pictures. This is an electronic board with a penlike device that is moved over its surface. The location of the pen sends coordinates to the computer so that a digital representation of the shape is captured in memory. The shape is also displayed on the screen. Joy sticks can be used to create shapes also, but this is a much cruder process.

Lines and shapes can also be created by software. Commands in BASIC, such as HLIN, VLIN, PLOT, permit the drawing of horizontal, vertical, and diagonal lines. Another programmatic technique is to create shape tables that define particular forms. The tables are accessed by programs to produce the stored shapes when required.

Color can be specified by using program commands. Alternatively, there are graphics keyboards that provide the user with thousands of color combinations through the use of special function keys.

Graphics is emerging as one of the exciting new areas of computing. Business people find that a picture is truly worth a thousand words. Artists are using graphics in advertisements. Educational aids and materials use graphics extensively. We are also seeing more and more of this emerging technology in movies and on television.

INTEGRATED SOFTWARE

Many of the preceding types of applications such as spreadsheets, word processors, and graphics came to the marketplace as stand-alone products. They are in widespread use for separate needs. There are occasions, however, when it's nice to be able to incorporate the spreadsheet data in a report that has been produced with word processing software. It's nice to be able to produce a graphics presentation directly from our data base files. These needs have led to the development of software that permits the integration of data from separate applications. Such software permits a finished product that begins to look suspiciously like our definition of information, in that it is both easy to understand and very useful to us.

Figure 4.8 Business graphics, courtesy of TeleVideo Systems, Inc.

5

Impact of Automation

EXPECTATIONS

The day has arrived, and the new system is sitting in the boxes in your office ready to be plugged in. What kind of experience are you in for? This all depends on the set of expectations you, the new user, have. Computers are very good at doing certain things. If your set of requirements lines up with the computer's capabilities, then you are in for a pleasant experience.

What are computers good at? They are very good at doing repetitive tasks. They will process a thousand invoices and never get bored. They are marvelous for linking information and for sorting it in the sequence the user specifies. They perform calculations without making arithmetic mistakes. They provide quick, easy access to information. You don't have to search through countless files and reports for the pieces of information you want. Computers permit you to enter a piece of data once and use it for many functions. These functions imply that you should experience a significant reduction in errors and processing time as you do your work.

On the other hand, since the computer does exactly what it is told, it does not compensate for things that it "should have known." If bad data is entered into the system, the computer will blithely add it to all the files it is instructed to. A data base can be contaminated with no trouble at all. The computer only makes the decisions it was programmed to make. The program may catch some of your errors if it is well written, but this generally means that it will check for type (alphabetic, numeric, etc.) and range (minimum and maximum values) or inclusion in a set. Therefore, situations that call for judgments, for making decisions, and for processing exceptions should be handled by people, not computers.

Computers do not solve management problems. If a business is out of control because of poor management practices, a computer can actually make things worse. This is true, as you can now appreciate, because the use of a computer requires structure and organization. Procedures must be followed for the operation and maintenance of the hardware, software, and data. A disorganized environment, fraught with interruptions and changes in policies and procedures is difficult, if not impossible, to computerize. This is not to say that a business drowning in paperwork should not be automated. If the source of the problem is an overload of redundant information handling, the solution is automation. If the requirement is for better access to information that is easy to computerize, you're on the right track in getting a computer.

ECSTASY AND RESIGNATION

From the above discussion, you probably realize that the computer is not the equivalent of the brain. You should probably be prepared for some wonderful surprises and some nasty shocks when you start using one. Since the computer does not deal with ambiguity very well, it cannot make the subconscious corrections that people make all the time. This produces an uneasy feeling in the beginning. You wonder what you'll do wrong next. Perfection is not a human state. There are a lot of rules to learn, and the computer requires that you learn them perfectly. If you remember that this kind of perfection is based on a rigid logic that must be obeyed, you will be able to accommodate to the totalitarian nature of the computer more comfortably. Actually, there is a certain security in a rigid structure that guarantees perfect repetition.

We need this assurance if we are going to turn the machine loose on our precious information. The speeds of the computer are beyond human comprehension, as we have learned. Therefore, we can do a great deal of useful work very quickly once we have ensured the correctness of the result.

Confusion is not a computer emotion. The machine will keep going, even if there is a logic error, until it cannot physically continue. This type of stoppage can occur for a number of different reasons, such as storage space used up, printer out of paper, operating system halt, or some other reason. It is up to human beings to design safeguards into the hardware and software to guard against logic flaws and other types of human error. The smarter we get about the dumb mistakes we can make, the better we get at designing fail-safe mechanisms.

Beyond building in protection from human error, we keep trying to make the computer behave in more "human" ways. We try to improve the conversational abilities of programs, to make them "user friendly." We output more messages to tell the user what's happening at a particular point and to instruct him as to what to do next. These are our beginning baby steps.

On the research front we explore topics like associative memory and artificial intelligence. We want to build more data connections; we want to make the machine function more like the brain. We are exploring the nature of human language with its associations and ambiguities. We want to make the computer speak.

Perhaps some day these things will be a reality. The fact is that computers today are still very dumb. Their saving grace is that they are very fast and infinitely patient. They require patience from you, the user (and a certain amount of resignation). After all, they really are nothing more than glorified adding machines. Do not expect miracles, and you probably will be very pleased (in time).

EMOTIONAL STAGES IN ACQUIRING A COMPUTER

Fear

The first stage experienced by almost all new computer owners is *fear*. It probably manifested itself well before the computer was actually delivered. In many cases it is left over from the feelings you experienced when the whole idea of getting a computer occurred to you in the first place. Now, there are compounding factors. You are confronted with a machine that you don't know how to use. Even if you've made a study of computers and understand all the theoretical information, you still have to learn the specifics of the one you've got. Each manufacturer and software house has its own procedures and instructions for operating its products. Of course, once you've learned how to use one computer, it's easier to learn a second, but it is a tedious process nevertheless. As a beginner you are afraid that you will break something, that you will lose your data, that you will appear stupid to others, that you will forget how to do something. The list goes on and on. There is the story about the new user who told me he was just sitting there "waiting for the thing to blow up."

At this stage the level of training and support from the vendor of your system can be very important. An even more critical factor is the quality of the documentation that comes with your system. If it is clear and has easy to understand examples and tutorials, then you can sit down with the manuals and teach yourself what you need to know in many cases. This does not include custom systems developed for your specific needs. The developer will have to teach you how the system works. If you are dealing with standard material and are not comfortable about teaching yourself, you can take courses in some of the more popular offerings, such as Wordstar and VisiCalc. For other needs you can hire someone to teach you. This may be the same consultant you used to help you select your system.

Your employees are just as frightened as you are. It is at this point that you'll be glad you let them participate in the initial system requirements definition. They now have a vested interest in seeing the thing work, too. These feelings must be capitalized on. You must set yourselves to the task of learning how to use your system. If you and your employees do not learn enough to get past the fear stage, chances are your system will sit in the corner gathering dust until you sell it to someone else, if you can. You will go around for quite a while saying uncomplimentary things about computers, to say nothing of feeling foolish and duped.

Accommodation

Once the initial hurdle is surmounted and you learn to use the computer, you will begin to experience the pleasure of having accurate, timely data. Annoying calculation errors will go away. The mounds of paper will start to disappear from the corners. Information will be available sooner. The invoices will be out on time. You will be able to find out about inventory levels and salespeople's productivity. You will actually get used to having current information. At this stage you will have accommodated to your system.

Dependence

The third stage is dependence. When your system is down your feelings will range from severe annoyance to utter frustration. Your business won't function very well when the system isn't working.

Even though you may have a manual fallback plan, doing all those things by hand will be such a nuisance that you will prefer to wait for the serviceman to fix the machine, if it isn't going to take too long. You won't be able to imagine how you ever got along without a computer.

You are now hooked. If you have to wait for the system to respond to your input, you will become very impatient. You will spend hours using the computer for functions you didn't realize you could accomplish in your pre-computer days.

Innovation

Soon you will begin to think of other things you would like to have. You will explore your system's more complex functions to see if you can implement your ideas. You will think creatively about the capabilities of the system to put your data together in new combinations. You will become aware of other programs you might wish to buy so you can do more. You may even learn to write your own programs. The things you cannot accomplish now will go into the "planning for the next system" category. You are now the master of your automated destiny.

CHANGE AND STRESS

The process that you will go through when you acquire a computer will put some stresses on your business. You should be prepared to accommodate to changes in the office procedures. Human beings resist change, especially if they are threatened by it. So the better you can prepare yourself and your employees for the changes, the more smoothly they will go. If job functions are going to change, the new assignments should be discussed with employees as early as possible. It will help if you know enough about what your system does to have planned for these changes before the hardware is actually plugged in. There may be a change in your forms. Perhaps your invoice and statement will look different. Reports from the system may now contain data that was filed in two or three different places before. It will take a little getting used to in order to be able to function comfortably with the new system.

You will have to learn to use and depend on the safeguards that are built into the system to verify your data. Most accounting systems, for example, give you the ability to batch financial transactions and use batch totals to verify that the data in the computer is accurate. The system may produce reports including daily listings of all transactions. Some systems require you to verify dollar amounts before the transactions are actually written to the files.

When you first acquire a system, it is a good idea to run parallel for a while. This entails doing all of the work the old way and also entering it on the computer. The results are then compared to see if the computer is getting things right. If this sounds like double work, it certainly is. You can cut over to the computer as soon as you are satisfied that you know how to use the system and that it is producing accurate data for you. If you have contracted for a custom system, it would be very unwise to accept it without running parallel for a little while.

TRAINING

You are not the only one who has to learn how to use the system. In fact, key employees may be the ones who learn first, rather than the boss. As we have said, learning happens mainly from manuals. If your contract stipulates a certain amount of training from the vendor, then this is how you and your employees will learn initially. It is usually not a good idea to train users in a new system's capabilities too early. You want to learn how to do something and then to practice doing it. So you don't want to schedule training before the system is available for practice.

You should plan for training. Allocate enough time and be sure the environment is conducive to concentrating on the new information. Do not expect to learn how to use a new system in the midst of the hubbub of ongoing office activities. If you can't afford to train all of your employees at once (sometimes the business has to go on), then select those who will learn quickly and who will be able to teach others. It is a good idea to train more than one person. You will want to have some backup in case of sickness or vacation, and so on.

If your employees have a positive attitude about the new system, it is amazing how much they will master, even if they are learning to use poorly designed, unfriendly systems. Pretty soon a new language will be spoken around the office, and you will notice a certain pride in being "computerized."

STORAGE AND BACKUP

You will now have to consider the management of your computerized files. If your information resides on floppy diskettes, you will need a filing system so that you can retrieve the diskette you need. It is a good idea to select names for your diskettes and for the files on them that are meaningful to you and others. Be sure to write the appropriate information on the stick-on label that comes with the diskette and to affix it to the cardboard cover. Write-protect tabs also come in the box of diskettes. For 8-in. diskettes, you put them on diskettes that you want to write to. For 5 1/4-in. diskettes, you put them on diskettes you don't want to write to. You should write-protect diskettes that contain programs and data that should not be changed or erased, such as copies of operating systems and read-only data files.

You should maintain a listing of the files on each diskette. Some systems allow you to print the directory of files for a diskette. You should do this when you finish adding or changing the information on a diskette. Record the date of the change. This procedure will ensure that you know which is the most current version of your data.

You should make copies of your data at periodic intervals. Backup procedures are a must to safeguard your data. This is true whether you use floppy disk or hard disk.

Since backing up all of the programs and data contained on a large capacity hard disk takes a while, especially if you are using floppy disks, you can set up a daily procedure to copy only the files that have changed, and do a complete backup once a week, or perhaps less frequently, if you feel that is sufficient. It is wise to have at least three sets of backups, the entire system (two complete copies, at a minimum), the latest incremental backup, and the second latest incremental backup. If you label the diskettes or tapes in sets, you can rotate the sets, writing over the oldest set with new information.

You should establish a backup procedure and stick to it. It is just when you get lazy about backing up that your system will go down, and you will have to reenter all the data that you created since your last backup. This can turn out to be an awful chore.

SUPPLIES

You will need to keep some supplies on hand for your computer. You will know how much of a certain item you need to stock after you use the system a while. The standard items include blank diskettes, tape cartridges, if you are using tape drives, and paper for the printer, including single-sheet supplies for letter quality output, forms such as invoices and statements, and plain continuous form paper for reports. You will need a supply of ribbons and a few print wheels or thimbles if you have a letter quality printer. One very important item is a diskette head cleaning kit. This is a special diskette made of scratchy material. It comes with a bottle of cleaning fluid. You pour a little of the fluid on the cleaning surface and insert the cleaning diskette in the drive. You close the door, and the drive head touches the cleaning surface. You leave the diskette in the drive for about 30 sec. so that any of the metal oxide coating that came off the data diskettes can be removed. You should plan to clean your drive heads at least once a week if you use diskettes heavily in your business processing.

THE PHYSICAL ENVIRONMENT

There are some environmental things computers don't like. They are allergic to dust, static, smoke, food, and beverages. Some businesses abuse their computers without realizing that these environmental pollutants will cause maintenance problems later on. Small business computers are built pretty ruggedly, so you're not going to destroy one if you have a cigarette now and then. After all, they are designed to be used in an office environment. But, if you want the best performance for your money, keep the environment as comfortable for your computer as you can.

You should have a separate power line for the computer. It should not be competing for power with the copier or the water cooler. A humidifier is a good idea if static electricity is a problem. There are antistatic sprays for carpeting.

Computers do best in moderate temperature ranges. If the temperature gets above 80°F, get an air conditioner, and put it on a separate circuit from the computer.

Space requirements are fairly flexible. Small business computers are fairly small, and many systems have modular components. Thus, they are pretty easy to place in an office. You do want to consider such things as sources of lighting and glare when placing CRTs. Naturally, you won't place your system next to the radiator.

Consider the furniture you plan to use. The height of the surface for the keyboard is very important. It should be low enough for the operator to be able to use the keyboard comfortably without getting back strain. This height varies with the individual, but it is usually at least 2 in. lower than the standard desk height. A good chair, with proper support for the back, is essential. It will cut down on back pain and fatigue.

SERVICE

Computers are very complex machines. Their parts are microscopic in size. It is not possible to open up the cabinet and fix things with a screwdriver. The day will come when your system will not do something you want to do. The first thing that will happen is that you will panic. If you have a service contract, you will then be able to "unpanic." Check to see that all the wires are plugged in, that all the switches are in the "on" position, and then try to do your activity again. If you are still unsuccessful, call the maintenance number. The service company will probably tell you to do the things that were just mentioned. It won't hurt to try again, but at this point you will know that something is probably wrong.

While there are some things that a serviceman can fix on-site, the most common form of service is to install a replacement part, such as a new CPU board or memory board, and send the old one back to the manufacturer for repair. Some service contracts include a swap provision which means that you get a replacement such as a CRT or printer while yours is being fixed. Sometimes the swap involves the entire system. This procedure ensures that you are not down for a period longer than it takes for the serviceman to get to your place of business and make the replacement. If you have hard disk and the failure is in the disk unit, you will be very glad that you stuck to your backup schedule because you will have to reload all of your programs and data onto the new disk in order to begin processing again.

You should find out what the service company guarantees for time to respond to a service call. There are sometimes different kinds of contracts you can take, depending on what time of day you need to have your machine available for processing. If your work hours are 9 to 5, then a normal work day contract will suffice. If you do your posting and billing at night on the second shift, then you would want an after hours contract. There are contracts that cover service 24 hours a day. Naturally, contracts outside the 9 to 5 hours are more expensive.

Maintenance contract costs are usually monthly fees based on a percentage of the purchase price of the equipment. They are usually signed for a year and then renewed.

If your vendor doesn't provide maintenance, you should ask if he knows who does. There are national companies, like Sorbus, that sell maintenance for some popular brands of microcomputers. If you can't get a maintenance contract on your intended system, you should consider very seriously whether or not this system is for you. There are carry-in service arrangements whereby you physically bring the "errant" component to a maintenance depot and leave it there to be fixed. There are a couple of hitches to be aware of in this scheme. First of all, the part that doesn't work may not be the one that's broken. A malfunctioning peripheral may be the result of a problem on the I/O board. There may be more than one problem in more than one component. Your alternative is to bring in the whole system to be checked out. That's feasible if you have more than one system so that you can still get some work done while your equipment is out for repair. If this is getting to sound more ridiculous by the moment, then carry-in maintenance is not for you. Actually, this form of service is really designed for the personal computer user who can be without computing power for a while until his system gets fixed.

HORROR STORIES

We are not going into specifics about horror stories. They really are a minute fraction of the sum total of computer experiences. You should be aware, however, that a very poorly designed computer system, particularly with respect to application software, can put you out of business. The major problem is that your business data gets so hopelessly garbled that you cannot unravel vital information about your customers and your money. Generally this happens in businesses that have such voluminous paperwork that it is not possible to recon-struct things from source documents. Again, this is a very rare occurrence.

More commonly, problems arise because the system is inadequate for the type and amount of processing it is used for, either because the system is too small or too slow, or because the programs are too inefficient. Poor program design, unclear or inadequate messages to the operator, complicated procedures for entering data—all of these things can cause discomfort without actually creating disaster.

It is hard to know what to say about service problems. They exist and you should be prepared for them. The serviceman will not always arrive within the specified contract period. It's a good idea to anticipate periods when you might be without a system and plan manual procedures that will let you con-tinue to take orders and do the other minimal activities that will keep you going until the system is up again.

PERSONALITIES

There is a certain personality profile that one might describe as being compati-ble with computers. This would be a person who is careful and methodical, who likes to pay attention to detail. The profile includes a self-starting attitude, a willingness to teach yourself, to ferret out information from manuals, a pro-pensity for looking up what you don't know. One major strength is the posses-sion of enough self-confidence to know that you can learn what you need to know and that you can find the information again once you know where it is documented. As a computer user you soon learn that there is simply too much information to keep in your head. You forget, particularly if you don't do a certain procedure very often. If you know where the instructions are for the activity you want to perform, you will be all right.

Patience is another very important characteristic for our computer per-sonality. It goes along with the careful, methodical approach. A liberal dose of creativity is very useful for figuring out how to organize procedures or how to use the data in new ways. Most small business people are, by nature, creative types, so this characteristic should be abundant in our hypothetical personality.

Since none of us possesses all of the characteristics we have mentioned, we can expect to run in to a few problems and to be a little unhappy sometimes.

BIG DECISIONS

If you have matched your system to your needs, you should feel very smart and very good rather soon after you get your computer. Things will become both easier and more interesting. You will be finished with the transactional work sooner. Your data will be more accurate and more current. You will have information that you never had before. All of this will give you better control over your business. You will be in a position to make better decisions. And you will be glad that you made that big decision for your small business.

6

The Search and
the Solution

A MULTIUSER CASE STUDY

The case study included here is presented to dramatize and highlight many of the points that are made in this book. The company and the characters are entirely fictional. The events are drawn in large part from actual happenings. Many of the events did occur in various situations and have been combined here for effect. Certain facts have been embellished upon to illustrate a particular concept. The process and the decisions are a fairly accurate representation of what happens when a business considers computerizing.

ACME Distributors, Inc.

ACME Distributors, Inc. is a wholesale distributor of watches. The president is Mr. Emerson, who founded the company about five years ago. He started in a modest fashion by using his home as his office and by making calls on prospective customers himself. Gradually the business grew. Then things really started to take off. Three years ago he leased office space, hired a salesperson named Ben and a very competent assistant named Prudence, who got the invoices and statements out and did the books. Prudence also handled any correspondence and took an occasional order over the phone.

Things got even better, and eventually Mr. Emerson decided he really should make a commitment to establishing and expanding his business. He began to advertise his products. He had to hire a full-time person to take the phone orders that came in. Her name was Jane. He also hired George to take care of the stock and to pack the orders for shipment. Soon the paperwork got to be too much for Prudence, so Mr. Emerson hired Gloria, fresh out of school to assist with the filing and billing. The latest member to join the current staff of ACME Distributors, Inc. was Mark, a hot-shot young salesperson whom Mr. Emerson hired about nine months ago.

Shortly after Mark was hired, Prudence went to Mr. Emerson and told him that she was overwhelmed by the paper work. She couldn't keep track of all the orders and invoices now that the company was doing so much business. Mr. Emerson asked her how much business that was. He said he really didn't have a good idea of how many invoices she had to handle. Prudence said she wasn't sure either, but she estimated that they had about 2000 customers, and they usually got 50 orders a day. After all, they were carrying lines from four different watch companies, and they had about 60 different styles. Of course at holiday time they had to hire two temps to help answer the phone calls because they could get up to 300 calls on any given day.

Mr. Emerson said that he was a little upset about the way the inventory was being managed, too. He had a hard time keeping track of what was selling well and what wasn't. He did all the buying for the company, and he knew

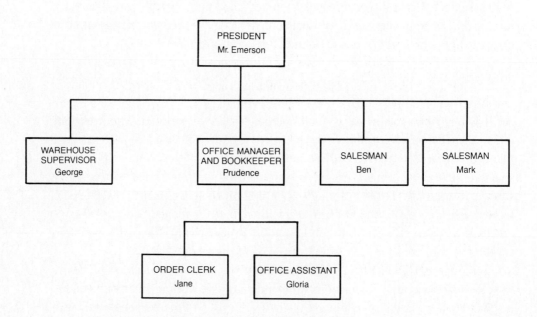

Figure 6.1 ACME Distributors, Inc. organization chart.

that sometimes they ran out of certain styles. Sometimes they had a lot of certain styles left. They discovered this situation when they did their physical inventory twice a year. Prudence suggested that he hire some more help.

Mr. Emerson thought this over and, being the progressive business person that he was, decided on a different alternative. He would get a computer. He had been reading all kinds of ads in the newspapers and magazines for computers. So a couple of days later, when he saw an ad for small business computers at special discount prices, he went to the computer store to see what they had. He told the salesperson about his problems with the paperwork and the inventory, and the salesperson told him they had just what he needed. He asked Mr. Emerson how many customers he had and how many orders he got each day. He did some quick calculations in his head and said that the double-sided double-density diskettes the system used would hold the customer and order files. All the operator would have to do would be to use a new diskette each month for orders. Their business system with two diskette drives and the heavy-duty printer was a very good buy right now. It came with a full set of business programs so that Mr. Emerson could do his payables, his payroll, and his general ledger, in addition to order entry, inventory control, and accounts receivable. The benefit of two disk drives was that the system could hold more information and that backing up files was much easier. They were offering a special 30-day trial period. If the customer wasn't satisfied within 30 days he could return the system and get a full refund, minus $100.

Mr. Emerson thought this all sounded great, although, perhaps a little overwhelming. He asked the salesperson to give him a demonstration. The salesperson showed him the main menu for the system which let the user select the function he wished to perform. They decided on "Enter Customer Information." Like magic, the next screen came up with a form to fill in for customer information. It had space for the name, address, bill to, ship to, and information like average purchase and year-to-date purchases. It even had information about delinquent payments. "Where does the financial information come from?" Mr. Emerson asked. The salesperson told him it was an integrated system which got information from the orders and the payments that were entered. It combined this data and produced the results he was seeing. This really seemed good to Mr. Emerson. And it was pretty cheap, only $6000. "How do we learn how to use it" was his next question. We have classes here at the store, the salesperson told him, or for an extra charge we can provide training at your place of business. "How long will it take to learn the system?" Mr. Emerson asked. The salesperson told him it was a one week course for each of the three major topics: Receivables, Payables, and Payroll/General Ledger. So Mr. Emerson decided that Prudence would be delighted, and he bought the system.

When he got back to the office and told Prudence about this, he was baffled by her response. He had never seen her so defensive before. She immediately began telling him how a computer simply wouldn't work. First of all, she had no time to leave the office to go to some silly classes. She had finished going to school a long time ago. She had heard that computers broke down a lot. Was he planning to get rid of Gloria? After all, computers replaced people. Or was he planning to let Gloria learn how to use the computer and fire her? Anyway, she was too old to learn how to use a computer.

Mr. Emerson realized that Prudence was terrified. But he still thought that once she became familiar with the computer, she would find that it helped her a lot. He hadn't considered firing her. She was much too important to him. He just didn't want to hire more people if he could help it. So he calmed her down and asked if she would use the computer on a trial basis. He would arrange with the store to have someone come to the office to train her and Gloria. They could send the computer back if they didn't like it.

Two weeks later the cartons arrived. The serviceman set the computer up, tested it out, and proclaimed it ready for use. Gloria went over and turned it on. She had used a computer in school and had some idea of how one worked. Then the phones started ringing, and Prudence told her to finish up the invoices she was working on because they had to go out that day.

The next day the man from the computer store came to begin to train Prudence and Gloria. He brought his 11-year old son, who was a computer whiz, with him. He began to demonstrate how to use the machine and how to load the programs. His son kept interrupting him whenever he didn't give a "complete" explanation of the facts about how the machine worked. The son also started talking about "head crashes" and "power spikes." It seems the computer was plugged into the general office circuit. "I hope you don't have a refrigerator on this circuit," the kid said. "I can't use my computer at home in the kitchen. The refrigerator knocked out the CPU."

Prudence knew she wasn't very happy. The phones kept ringing and there were statements to get out, and she had to get to the bank before it closed. Besides, Gloria seemed very interested in this computer. She was asking all kinds of questions.

The next day the man from the store called to say that he couldn't make it. He had an appointment at an account the store had just sold 20 computers to. They had arranged a special training session for their employees and the person who was supposed to teach the course was sick. He would see them next week.

On Monday training resumed. For the first hour things seemed to be going pretty well. Gloria entered some orders while Prudence looked over her shoulder and watched. There was only one terminal so they had to take turns. Prudence was glad that Gloria wanted to enter the orders because she didn't want to look foolish if she made a mistake. On the other hand, there were certain things that she had always taken care of like adjusting the price for special discounts that she knew certain customers got. Gloria didn't know about this. The instructor told her they could enter a special discount in the customer record. The problem was that Mr. Emerson made a new price for his special customers most of the time and it was never the same. Well, they could override the price that the system calculated, he told her. What was the point of having the system calculate the price if they had to enter another one, she wanted to know.

This thing was beginning to feel very restricting to Prudence. She was wondering how she and Gloria were going to be able to use the system together. It looked like she would have to wait until Gloria entered all the orders before she would be able to enter the payments. Unless she let Gloria do all the work. She didn't see how everything would get done, especially around holiday time when they really got busy.

She also wanted to know how the information was organized. How could she find out about overdue balances? The instructor explained that the system kept track of running balances in the customer record. If she wanted to know the details of any particular purchase she would have to load the order diskette for the month in question to look them up. Prudence said that she didn't always know which month she needed to look up for her information. This seemed to be a little inconvenient. They already had enough trouble finding invoices, and she thought the computer was supposed to make things better.

The instructor kept telling her that it was important to read the manuals to understand how the system worked. She worked hard enough as it was. She didn't have any time to read the manuals. It all seemed very confusing. There were so many things to remember, and the constant interruptions made it impossible to concentrate. Instead of helping, the computer was making things worse. The paper work was piling up while she was spending time with this foolish thing. George had just called to ask where the invoices were so that he could get his shipments out. Wasn't it bad enough that they were always at least three weeks late shipping their orders? Now, she was delaying him even more! If that wasn't bad enough Mark, the hot-shot salesperson, had also called, complaining that his commission was wrong again and that one of his customers had been billed twice. Prudence though it was probably one of those problems they had occasionally when the customer called the office after the salesperson had also written the same order. This happened when the customer got impatient.

The next day the store called to say they were terribly sorry, but the instructor had taken a job with his brother-in-law in the automobile business and they didn't have anyone to send for training. Prudence was actually quite relieved.

She went in to Mr. Emerson's office and told him that the computer was not going to work. It was too complicated, it was delaying their work, and it couldn't do the things they needed it to for their business. She was so definite in her statements that Mr. Emerson called up the computer store and told them to come and get the machine.

Mr. Emerson was plainly baffled. He thought that computers were supposed to be wonder machines. Everything had certainly sounded good at the computer store. Where had they gone wrong?

A few months later, Mr. Emerson was attending the annual industry convention. He noticed that one of the sessions featured a speaker on business automation. The panel also included two wholesalers whose companies had computerized. He listened to the speaker talk about the process of analyzing the needs of a business in order to determine its computer requirements. He talked about determining the objectives of the business person; what did he want to accomplish; what were his goals. After that one set the scope of the project. How big was it? How much did the business person want to accomplish? This was determined in part by certain constraints that might apply, like cost, manpower, space, and so on. Priorities were set with the most critical needs ranked highest. These functions would be implemented first.

After that the speaker discussed the detailed analysis phase. In this phase, one took a very careful look at the way the business operated. The procedures and forms were examined; the data used in the company's daily operations was reviewed. The staff was interviewed. The speaker said this was particularly important to give employees the feeling of participating in the project and to begin to deal with the fear of computers that most people harbored. Mr. Emerson realized that, on this point at least, he had certainly made a mistake. He had never even consulted Prudence, or anyone else, about the computer. It had not occurred to him to do it.

The speaker continued with his description of the process. After a careful analysis of current procedures, the objectives were examined and requirements were determined. Software and hardware to satisfy the requirements and to enable the business to meet its needs was specified. The speaker said that it was very important to get the right size system for the business. It had to be large enough to hold all the required information and to permit easy access to such information. On the other hand, it didn't have to be very large if a small system was all that was required. He said it took some experience to be able to determine need and size and to translate manual functions to computerized ones. He said it was wise to work with a knowledgeable dealer or consultant. He also mentioned such things as training, support, and service.

After the speaker was through, Bill Smith, one of Mr. Emerson's biggest competitors, spoke about how his computer had absolutely turned his business around. He talked about mountains of paper, late and lost invoices, poor inventory control, payroll problems, and so on, that had all but disappeared since he had computerized. In addition to cleaning up the problems, he said that he had been able to enlarge his business 20 percent in the last six months without hiring any more employees. This was pretty upsetting to Mr. Emerson. He was just as good a business person as Smith. The problems certainly sounded familiar, though.

That night at the cocktail party, Mr. Emerson approached Bill Smith. "Say, Bill," he opened, "how did you happen to get into this computer thing?" "Well," Smith answered, "I saw this ad in the newspaper for small business computers. I had really been having a lot of problems in the office getting out the paperwork, and I never seemed to have the right kind of information about my inventory or my salespeople. So I said to myself, why not get a computer. I talked it over with my office manager, and she said her friend worked in an office where they had just gotten a computer. She said they had used a consultant and they were very happy with their system. So she got the name of the consultant, I called the company to check on him, and then I called him in. He went around and poked his nose into every aspect of my business. He talked to all the key employees, and then he came up with this plan for us. So far we've been really pleased, as I mentioned in my talk."

"I'm thinking of computerizing, too," Mr. Emerson said. "Would you recommend that I use your consultant? I know my business is smaller than yours, but we seem to be having the same problems you had."

"Of course, I would. I think computers are great for businesses with our kinds of problems. Why don't you call me as soon as we get back home, and I'll give you his name and phone number."

Not long afterwards, Mr. Emerson had his first meeting with Martin Anderson, the computer consultant. He mentioned the abortive attempt at computerizing that ACME had made, and Martin said that such unfortunate experiences were all too common. He said he wanted to discuss Mr. Emerson's reasons for getting a computer, and then he would take a close look at the business to see if, in fact, ACME would benefit from computerizing.

Mr. Emerson wanted to know how much it would cost for Anderson's services. They discussed a daily fee of $350. Anderson said that he could quote a fixed price based on his estimate of the time it would take to do the job once he had spoken to Mr. Emerson, if that was preferable. He said his services included an analysis of the business and its data processing requirements, an investigation of existing software and hardware to see what would be applicable to ACME's needs, help in selecting the software and hardware from alternatives if there were several, help with the installation, and training. He said he usually worked with the hardware dealer that was selected as far as hardware installation went. He didn't sell any hardware himself. Mr. Emerson wanted to know what happened if Anderson couldn't find existing software. Anderson said his company did customize applications when required. They preferred to use data base management software because this provided the user with a great deal of flexibility in accessing his data once the system was implemented. He said it was also very easy to make changes and add information in a data base management system. For standard accounting needs he said there were many good packages already available on the marketplace.

Mr. Emerson began to list the reasons why he wanted a computer, his objectives, as Martin called them. First of all, he felt that he wasn't really on top of his inventory. He could go in and eyeball the stock any time, but he often ran out of items and sometimes he got stuck with slow sellers and took a beating. He also wanted to have a better idea of how his salespeople were doing. He knew he had to do something about making his receivables more current, too. He thought if he could collect the money from customers before it became too long overdue, he'd have a better chance of collecting it altogether. There were also periods when he had to borrow from the bank to finance inventory, and if he could plan his cash flow a little better, he might be able to reduce some of his financing. Of course, he wanted to increase his business. He would like to take on some new products in addition to watches, but right now they had all they could do to handle the products they sold. One idea he had had for a long time was to publish a catalog and do some mail-order business.

Martin Anderson said that these were all classic reasons for computerizing a business, and that it seemed that Mr. Emerson was right in thinking of doing so. He said he would like to speak to the key employees to get more information about the details of how ACME actually functioned on a daily basis. He said that Mr. Emerson was also a key employee and that he would come back to talk to him again after he had spoken to the others.

The first person Martin Anderson interviewed was Prudence. He told her that he knew about the unfortunate experience that ACME had had with a computer. He asked her to tell him what her feelings were about computers in general and about their unhappy experience, in particular. Prudence admitted that she was afraid of computers. They seemed very complicated, and she was afraid she wouldn't be able to learn how to use one. From what she could see the computer wasn't going to help ACME anyway. It didn't do the things they needed. Anderson asked her to explain what she meant. She talked about the way ACME, or rather, Mr. Emerson, did business. He makes a special price almost every time he makes a sale. We would have to change the price the computer calculated most of the time. Anderson mentioned that the computer did do a lot of the other repetitive work like retrieving customer information and product descriptions automatically for the orders and invoices. Prudence admitted that those were nice features. She launched into a discussion of her view of the business problems.

"Mr. Emerson only deals with the large customers. Ben and Mark handle our smaller volume, regular customers. And we get a lot of phone orders from intermittent customers. There are lots of problems with orders. Often we can't find the back invoices for a customer, so Mr. Emerson has to rely on his memory for the last prices he quoted. He also has to remember what the latest price of the watches he's selling was, unless he happens to have the bills in front of him. He's really good at this most of the time. He did make a mistake with one of our biggest customers once, and they got pretty mad. It seems they had a computer and knew what they had paid on the last order. He wasn't sure of his prices and said he'd have to call them back. This business runs on personal contact a lot. There are an awful lot of watch dealers out there. Mr. Emerson eventually got the thing straightened out, but the orders from the other company are not what they were.

"Ben is a wonderful salesperson. He doesn't make a lot of noise, but he always has his paperwork in, and his customers like him a great deal. Mark, our new man, is another story. It seems like he makes an awful lot of mistakes. For some reason, his customers seem to get a lot of double bills and a lot of double orders. We do have a problem once in a while when the customer calls up to order something that he has also ordered from the salesperson. Jane, our regular order taker, is very good at asking the customer if the salesperson already took the order. She tells the customer that the order will be shipped shortly. We are a little behind in getting our shipments out, so sometimes the customer gets impatient and phones in the order again. Anyway, Jane tells him the merchandise is on the way. When we have temps at peak periods, double orders sometimes get past us. The invoices are in the pipeline somewhere, either waiting for Gloria to type them, or in the warehouse waiting for George to send them out with the merchandise. So we can't always check to see if an order has been placed.

"We try to keep up with the paperwork, but we sometimes fall behind. Once in a while we just simply lose an invoice. We try to keep track of them by logging them in this book, but sometimes we goof. We file three copies of the invoice as it is, and it's easy to misplace one."

Martin Anderson wanted to know why they file three copies of each invoice. Prudence told him that they filed one copy by date. When a payment came in, they pulled that copy, marked it paid, and filed it in the customer's folder. This was the way they aged their receivables. They tried to go through the file by date at least once a month to send late notices and call accounts that were delinquent more than 60 days. The second copy was filed by invoice number. The third one went into the customer's folder and was replaced by the copy marked paid, if and when the invoice was paid. When a payment came in, if the invoice number was on the face of the check, they could locate the invoice in the invoice number file and find out the date to pull the invoice in the date file. If they didn't have the invoice number, they looked up the invoice in the customer's file. Mr. Anderson mentioned that it seemed they were doing quite a bit of filing. Prudence agreed. She said they needed all their current files to find their records, though. Anderson remarked that one of the main functions of a computer was to let the user get at information quickly and easily. He said that a computer system should permit the user to look up an invoice by customer name, customer number, if there was one, invoice number, or date. The information was only filed once and was accessed by "keys," that is, the fields of information he had just mentioned. This way there was no problem about duplicate copies and misfiling or losing an item. The computer typically assigned invoice numbers sequentially so the user did not have to worry about what the next number was supposed to be. "You mean I wouldn't have to look in three different places to find an invoice?" Prudence asked. She liked that idea a lot.

Anderson continued by telling her that, in addition to letting you access your information easily, computers let you keep track of information. Most accounts receivable programs automatically age your receivables. You can print out a list of overdue customers whenever you like. They also accumulate total sales-to-date for customers so you know how much business they're doing with you. "Why didn't the computer trainer tell me this?" Prudence asked. Anderson said it sounded like they hadn't gotten that far with him.

"Now that you are beginning to see how a computer functions, what other uses do you think you might have for one?" Anderson asked. He was careful not to talk about "what other *problems*" Prudence might have. The typical answer to that was that things were fine and there weren't any problems, only a few inconveniences, but nothing that more help couldn't solve.

Prudence said that knowing about delinquent accounts sooner would certainly help, especially if they had a list that they could call from. They had had to write off several bad debts last year because they had let things slip past 120 days and at that point it was almost impossible to collect any money.

She said she didn't know if this was possible, but it would be nice to be able to track response to advertising. ACME spent a great deal on advertising in various newspapers and magazines and it was hard to know which ads were pulling and which weren't. If they were deluged with phone calls after a particular ad appeared, they knew that particular one was a winner. Anderson said this was certainly possible on a computer.

"Can the computer do statements?" Prudence asked. "Yes," Anderson said. "If the order entry function is automated, that is, if the order is entered directly into the computer, then invoice preparation can also be automatic. Statements are usually produced automatically from the information entered into the computer when an order is taken, when an invoice is generated, and when payments are applied. Some firms don't automate the order entry function. They only enter invoices into the system to use the receivables function.

The receivables still keep track of what was billed and what was paid and what is outstanding. The order entry part precedes the receivables function, as Prudence knew because that was what she did first in her manual system now. "It seems to me that order entry on the computer would be very useful to us," she said. Prudence was now beginning to participate in the planning stage. She was thinking of ways that a computer could help her, functions that she wanted from a computer. This was just what Anderson had hoped for. If she had a part in the planning she would have an investment in using a system to satisfy her needs.

"I would like to see your forms and your books," Anderson asked. Prudence wanted to know what for. "The data that an organization uses must go into computer files if it is to automate. Most companies of your type take orders, send invoices and statements, and record their payments in much the same way. That is why there are standard accounting programs on the market. Still no two companies are exactly alike. Your desire to track the results of your advertising, for example, is something that all companies don't want to do. I want to see if there are other things that you might need that a standard package won't supply."

Anderson looked at the order forms, the invoices, the statements, and the "books," including the cash journal and the check register. He didn't see anything very different from standard business procedures. The payroll was done manually, but since the number of employees was quite small this didn't seem unusual. "I notice that you draw checks for employees other than their paychecks. Why is that?" he asked.

Prudence said that sometimes the commissions were miscalculated because of the lost order problem, and Mr. Emerson didn't want the salespeople to have to wait for the next paycheck if the company had made a mistake. Prudence said the men weren't so quick to report double payments, though, especially Mark.

It was really a nuisance to keep track of lost orders where the commissions had already been paid, though. It occurred to Prudence that if the orders weren't "lost" this burdensome task would go away. She was beginning to think that maybe she had been a little hasty in her evaluation of computers. They'd have to show her how the thing worked, though, before she would go along with it.

Anderson said she'd been enormously helpful and that he was going to speak to the other members of the staff. Did she think Gloria had anything to add. Prudence had to admit that she had been upset by the way Gloria seemed to take to computers, but as long as he was asking her. . . . After all, Gloria was going to have to enter the orders if they got a computer. And if the orders were done correctly, that would mean less work later on for her. So she said she thought Gloria would be able to help with her area of responsibility, the orders and invoices.

Anderson found Gloria a delight to talk to. She knew a little bit about computers and really believed that a computer would help ACME. She said she and Prudence often worked late to get out the invoices. George really gave it to them when they were way behind. Of course, they were always at least three weeks behind, and some of the customers were getting pretty impatient. It hadn't always been like that, but the number of orders had been much smaller until recently. She figured she typed 50 to 75 invoices a day. Sometimes Prudence helped her, and occasionally they got a temporary typist in if they were really behind. She said that she thought she could learn how to use a computer pretty quickly. She did mention that there seemed to be a problem with the other computer they had gotten. She thought it would be a problem to have to look up orders separately by month, since they often needed to go back 60 or 90 days to find what they were looking for.

Gloria said she knew that computers had word processing functions, and she thought that would be something they could use. They sent notices to their customers about special purchases and there were the usual letters and things.

Martin Anderson went into the warehouse which adjoined the offices to talk to George. George was surprised that Anderson wanted to talk to him. He had some things to say, all right. He was trying to do a good job for ACME, but the conditions he was working under were making it almost impossible. They were so far behind lately that it looked like they would never catch up. With the potential ACME had, he should be able to keep two more people busy packaging orders. But because of the bottleneck in the office, he only got enough invoices every day to keep himself busy. He knew that there were double shipments sometimes but he couldn't tell from the invoices whether a customer had ordered more items or whether the office had just duplicated the original order. Ever since Mark came to work for ACME he thought there seemed to be more double orders. Ben's customers didn't seem to get as many of them.

At this point a man walked up to Anderson and George. "Hi, Ben," George said. "Meet Mr. Anderson. He's the computer consultant that Mr. Emerson hired to come in and look us over." Ben and Mark spent most of the month on the road, but Ben happened to be in town. He had a special rush order for one of his best customers, and he had come to the warehouse to see if they had the inventory on hand to ship. The two men went over to a shelf in the rear of the warehouse, and Anderson heard Ben say that he would tell Emerson to order more of that style. He knew there was an order for all of the current stock waiting on Gloria's desk to be typed, but he needed what they had right away. George said something about "here we go again."

Martin Anderson asked Ben if he could spare a few minutes to talk. Ben said sure, why didn't they grab a bite of lunch. Over lunch Ben told Anderson that he really liked working for Emerson. He was a fair guy, even if he was a little disorganized. He thought that was because the business had grown so fast, and they really hadn't planned for so much volume. Anderson asked him if there was information that he could use that he didn't have now. Ben said the most important thing for him would be to know when his customers' orders had been shipped. The clerks were so far behind that they couldn't even give him a list of his monthly sales. They calculated his commissions from the orders he sent in, so he had to keep his own lists to double check. If one of his customers called in an order in between his visits, he was supposed to get a commission anyway, but the clerks slipped up on this once in a while. He also said that it was getting hard to tell his customers when they would receive their merchandise. Something had to be done to handle the purchasing of inventory better.

Anderson asked if Mark were in town, too. Ben said he didn't know. They had different territories, and he rarely saw Mark. "One more question," Anderson said. "Do you have a lot of trouble with double orders?" "Not really," Ben answered. "Once in a while it happens, but I usually know what my customers want and when they want it."

The next day Martin Anderson had another meeting with Mr. Emerson. He said that the employees had been very cooperative and helpful and that he just wanted to clear up a few things before he went off to analyze the requirements of ACME as far as computerizing was concerned. He asked about the purchasing procedures. Mr. Emerson said that he thought things could probably be done in a more organized fashion. It seemed that they did quite a bit of juggling with the inventory to fill priority orders. This was why he was doing the purchasing himself. If the process were smoother, and Prudence weren't so busy, she could probably handle the purchasing of the stock. She purchased all of the office supplies and other items that ACME bought anyway.

The last item Anderson wanted to discuss was the pricing policy. Was it necessary to set a different price most of the time? Emerson said he didn't know. He was trying to give quantity discounts and still make his profit margins. The problem was that the costs of his merchandise changed pretty often, and he was trying to estimate price to keep within his profit guidelines. Since he didn't have time to really sit down with his purchase orders and do the calculations, he found that he was guessing a lot of the time.

Anderson thanked him for his time and frankness and said he would call in two weeks with his report and proposal. Mr. Emerson asked him if he thought a computer would help ACME. "Enormously" was the response.

True to his word, Martin Anderson returned in two weeks with a written analysis and proposal for computerizing ACME. Included in the document was a list of the objectives that ACME wanted to fulfill, a statement of the requirements for software and for hardware, and an estimate of what a typical system might cost. Anderson discussed these items with Mr. Emerson.

Objectives in Their Order of Priority

1. Reduce paperwork and processing time.
2. Reduce billing errors.
3. Improve inventory management.
4. Improve collections.
5. Get better information on salesperson productivity.
6. Get better information on sales, cash flow, profitability.
7. Keep staff increases to a minimum.
8. Increase product line.
9. Produce a catalog

Mr. Emerson agreed that those were the objectives he thought were important.

Anderson said they could develop a set of requirements from the list of objectives. They had also defined the order of implementation by setting priorities. He mentioned that the items at the top of the list dealt with order entry and accounts receivable functions. These functions could be satisfied with many good standard accounting packages. As a result of using a package, the paperwork that Prudence and Gloria did would be reduced. The system would automatically produce invoices once the orders were released for processing. Anderson suggested that they put a printer in the warehouse so that George could start work from the invoices as soon as they were ready. As far as taking orders was concerned, Jane could input the phone orders directly into the system from a terminal. Since the customer information would be on the computer, she could check right away for information like credit limits and delinquent accounts to know whether or not to take the order. Gloria could put in the mail orders at another terminal. There was a way to help Ben and Mark, too. They could have portable terminals which hook up to the telephone. This way they could call up the computer at their convenience and enter their orders directly. The system would advise them about delinquencies and over credit limits, too. They will also be able to find out when their outstanding orders had been shipped. And they would be able to get information on their sales to date and commissions. "Wait a minute," said Mr. Emerson, "I don't mind if they find out how they're doing individually, but there is certain information that is none of their business, like how profitable we are, or what some of the other employees' salaries are." Anderson explained that the system he had in mind had priority access levels built into it. The system supervisor, who would probably be Prudence, could set up passwords and access rights to various information. This was done by assigning certain priorities to individual passwords. An individual could only access files that were at his level of priority and that were assigned to his password.

Anderson continued with the benefits of the software, mentioning that ACME would be able to eliminate double billing, would have current information on orders processed and invoices produced which would almost eliminate double orders, and would have an inventory management function which would let them set reorder points so that the system would automatically notify them when the inventory was low. An aged receivables function would automatically list accounts delinquent 30, 60, and 90 days. Reports would be available for salesperson productivity.

Once the order entry and receivables function was installed and working, ACME could install a General Ledger function. This would produce an income statement showing a summary of income and expense and the net profit or loss. It would also produce a balance sheet showing assets and liabilities which would provide Mr. Emerson with information about the condition or health of his business. These reports could be produced whenever he wanted them. The information would be automatically generated from the receivable function because the accounts would be set up according to the ones used in the General Ledger. Payables and Payroll account figures could be entered into the General Ledger manually by Prudence, or ACME could buy software to automate these functions and automatically feed the General Ledger. This was the purpose of an integrated system that knew about common files and shared them. The payroll was quite small and probably could be handled manually for a while, but the option for automating it if the company got very large was available by going with an integrated package.

Once the system was producing the totals that the business required, Mr. Emerson would be able to use an electronic spreadsheet program to track his profitability. He could do budgets and track actual sales against them. He could project the percentage of profitability he wanted and calculate how much business he would have to do at specific prices, given specific costs to meet his goals. This information really amazed Mr. Emerson. He really hadn't thought about using the computer himself. He confessed that he didn't know if he could. Anderson assured him that he would have no trouble at all. Part of the training service he provided included showing the boss how to use an electronic spreadsheet.

Anderson continued with a discussion of the word processing requirements for ACME. In addition to the catalog, you have the usual letters and notices and you also send special mailings to your high-volume customers. A word processing program will help you to do these things efficiently. If you want a typeset catalog with pictures, you can still prepare the text portions yourself. This would include any pricing and price changes that come along. You can then either give the typesetter a floppy diskette if his computer can read yours, or you can transmit your data to him via a communications link. The typesetter won't have to enter the data again, and this should save you enough money to cover the cost of the communication, and then some.

In order to keep track of responses to your advertising, we could set up a small data base. You would enter data about the ads and the responses, and the system would count how many, how much, and any other information you wanted. The advantage of using a data base is that you can use the data in it as you desire. You are not restricted to the formats that the already designed programs produce. As long as we put all the data you need in the data base, you can count and total and design your own reports based on any or all of the fields in the data base.

"You mean if I have some harebrained scheme in the future, we could put it on the data base to keep track of too?" Mr. Emerson asked. Anderson said it didn't work quite that way. If the "harebrained scheme" involved collecting organized, repetitive data, then the answer was yes. If the scheme involved something that was very changeable and involved a lot of judgments and decision making, then the answer was probably no. The reason that ACME was so suited for computerization now was that the type of information the business required lent itself readily to the way computers processed data. Anderson said that he was able to match almost all of ACME's requirements to available software and hardware offerings.

There was one issue, however, that he would like to discuss. This was the practice of setting a separate price for almost every sale. Most accounts receivable systems provided the capability for a certain number of pricing levels. Customers could be coded for certain levels, and quantity sales could be coded at certain prices. If these conventions were followed, then the system would automatically calculate the extension, that is, the total amount due for each product. There generally was an override capability, but this meant more work for the data entry operator, and it also reduced the effectiveness of reports on profitability calculations. If Mr. Emerson could manage to set up six pricing levels or so, the system could handle his calculations very nicely. Mr. Emerson said that he would actually prefer to deal with a set number of pricing levels. That way he wouldn't have to be guessing every time he quoted a price. If he had current information about profit margins, fixed price levels wouldn't be any problem at all.

Mr. Emerson wanted to know about adding new products to his product line. Anderson said that should be very easy once a system was set up. It was simply a matter of adding more products to the product file. It was also a simple matter to delete products from the product file. They would not be available for any further sales once they were deleted. The descriptions would have to stay on the file to provide the information for past orders, but that would be all.

Anderson showed Mr. Emerson a list of his software requirements:

1.   Standard accounting package
      Modules needed immediately:
            Order Entry
            Inventory Control
            Accounts Receivable
            General Ledger
      Future modules:
            Accounts Payable
            Payroll
2.   Word processing software (including mailing list and label generation)
3.   Spreadsheet program
4.   Data base manager
5.   Communications software

Anderson said that another very important piece of software was the operating system that was responsible for running the entire system, both software and hardware. That was usually included in the price of the hardware. Anderson estimated that the cost of packaged software would be $5000 to $6000. In addition, it would be $2500 to develop a customized data base for ACME.

They talked about hardware requirements next. The most important items to consider when deciding on a hardware configuration were how much data had to be stored and whether or not more that one person needed to access the same files at the same time. The number of orders and the other activities that ACME must perform during the day indicated that they needed a multi-user system. This would permit order entry, invoice and statement creation, word processing, and analysis and modeling to go on simultaneously. If each activity had to be performed one after the other, at a minimum, the orders and the invoices would collide with each other. There wouldn't be enough time to get everything done with a single-user system. Mr. Emerson remarked that the first system he had brought wouldn't have worked for them then, would it. Anderson told him that on the basis of use alone it would not have. In addition there was another problem. The first system didn't have enough disk storage. According to Anderson's calculations ACME needed at least 13 million bytes or characters of disk storage right now, and that was allowing for only moderate expansion. If they were going to have a multiuser system then the files that any user needed would have to be available. Clearly they couldn't be switching diskettes between word processing and spreadsheet analysis while they were trying to take orders and print invoices. In addition, there might be more than one order taker on the system at the same time, especially in peak periods. Each one needed access to all the files. The plan to put each month's orders on a separate diskette showed a certain failure to appreciate the way an office handled its work. Theoretically it was possible. Practically it was inefficient and burdensome for the operators, to say the least.

According to Anderson's calculations of the record sizes for the various files, the number of records in each file, and an allowance for moderate business expansion, ACME's disk requirements were as follows:

Customer file—2500 customers × 200 bytes	500,000
Product file—100 products × 75 bytes	7,500
Invoice file—2500 customers × 2 orders/month × 150 bytes × 12 months	9,000,000
Cash journal—5000 payments × 50 bytes	250,000
Word processing files	1,000,000
Spreadsheets	250,000
Programs and system software	1,500,000
Total bytes	12,507,000

This list shows that you need a hard disk capability on any system that you would be considering. Hard disk comes in specified increments depending on which computer manufacturer we decide to go with. Usually the smallest size is 5 million bytes. The next size is somewhere around 18 to 20 million bytes, and capacity increases from there to 40 million, 60 million, and so on. Since 5 million is too small, we should consider the next size which would be 18 to 20 million bytes. That will give you plenty of room for expansion and current work space. "Isn't it wasteful to buy so much more than you need?" Mr. Emerson asked. Anderson said it tended to fill up pretty quickly, and the price difference in the sizes was only about $1000 to $1500.

Total Hardware Needs

Multiuser central processing unit with a minimum of 512K of memory
1 floppy disk drive (for loading programs and backing up files)
3 CRT terminals with detachable keyboards for data entry
(2 to be shared by Jane, Gloria, and Prudence,
1 for spreadsheet analysis, temps, backup, etc.)
2 portable terminals with hardcopy output for salespeople
1 remote dot matrix printer for invoices in the warehouse
1 letter quality printer for statements and correspondence
communications connections and modems
Streaming tape unit for file backup (optional)

Anderson said that he had made some rough price estimates for the hardware on the list. The streaming tape unit was something ACME could wait for. They could try backing up with floppy disks. If they found that it was taking too long they could always get the streamer. The prices looked like this:

CPU with 1 floppy drive	$ 3,000
3 terminals @ $1000 each	3,000
2 portable terminals @ $1000	2,000
Hard disk drive	3,500
Dot matrix printer	1,800
Letter quality printer	3,000
Communications	3,500
Total	$19,800
Maintenance contract	
1 1/2% /month = $297	3,564
Streaming tape $3,500	

As Mr. Emerson could see, this was considerably more than the $6000 bargain that he had wanted. He told Anderson that $22,000 was more than he had anticipated. Anderson asked him to think about the alternatives. Not only would he have to hire more people, but also he would not solve his inventory control problem which was probably costing him several thousand dollars a year. Could he estimate how much lost business he was incurring because of late deliveries? What were his finance costs to borrow to finance inventory because of his cash flow problems? How much did he write off in delinquent accounts? Didn't he say it was thousands of dollars? Considering these items alone a computer system would be cost justified in the first year.

The prices estimated here were for a microcomputer, which was much less expensive than a minicomputer system would be. Since ACME didn't need the large, sophisticated, multiuser file handling and communications capabilities of a minicomputer system, Mr. Emerson didn't have to consider a price tag upwards of $40,000. The present solution was not excessively costly for the requirements. It would provide additional benefits which would let ACME expand. It was very hard to estimate how much the capability to expand a business was worth, but the amount would be in addition to the justification based on immediate problems that they were eliminating.

Martin Anderson told Mr. Emerson that he would like him to see a demonstration of a system that was similar to the one he needed. "Do you mean Bill Smith's system," Emerson asked. "No," said Anderson. "His business has different requirements from yours. He has offices in several cities and he ships from four warehouses located in different parts of the country. He has one of those large minicomputer systems we were discussing. The system I want you to see is one I put in for a client about two years ago. His business is a little different from yours, and it doesn't have the growth potential yours does. Therefore the hardware I am looking for for you will be a little different from what he has, but you will be able to see all of the software functions we discussed, and you will see a multiuser system in action."

Mr. Emerson wanted to know a little more about how Anderson was going to select hardware. Anderson said that he dealt with several very reputable dealers who provided good support and service. They sold nationally known brands of equipment. If they went out of business, national service companies also provided maintenance on the hardware.

Anderson continued to explain that microcomputers were just coming of age for small business use. This meant that multiuser operating systems were being developed and supported by various vendors. The previous emphasis had been placed much more on the individual user. Software was also coming to the market to run on these newer systems. The client they were going to see had a small operation. He didn't need to have more than one person taking orders and accessing his business files at one time. Since word processing ran under separate programs and used different files, the man could do both business processing and word processing on his machine simultaneously. Therefore, he had two terminals on his system, but he didn't do any file sharing. Mr. Emerson's volume was such that he would need to have both Gloria and Jane, and maybe even Prudence, entering orders and doing other business functions simultaneously. So he needed a full-fledged multiuser system. But the demo would show him the logic of the programs in action.

Anderson suggested that Prudence come along also. She might have some procedural questions to ask. The demonstration was very reassuring to both Prudence and Mr. Emerson. They actually saw a computer processing data in procedures that looked a lot like their business. They got an idea of the flow of information, and the sequence of activities that were performed. They saw the invoices and the statements, and they were reassured about how much easier life had become with the acquisition of the computer.

Mr. Emerson felt confident about the move he was contemplating. "O.K.," he said, "when do we start?" Anderson suggested that Mr. Emerson gather the employees together at a meeting to tell them that he was willing to get a computer and to discuss their ideas, fears, and concerns. He said he would like to be there to answer questions and to discuss the conversion effort that would be required to put ACME's data on the computer before they could start using it. He thought it would be a good idea to let the people involved help in estimating how much time it would take. Additionally, he would like to discuss the changes in procedures and job functions that the computer would cause.

He would also like to discuss training. It would be better if it could be done at his facility away from the ongoing activities in the office. Perhaps they could work out a schedule so that Gloria and Prudence could be trained during slack time. Then they could back each other up and train anyone else who needed training.

ACME proceeded with the computer project. The installation, training, and conversion went pretty smoothly. Once in a while there was a question or some confusion, especially in the beginning, but on the whole it was a successful effort.

The invoice problem cleared up nicely. Customers didn't complain; George got his shipments out the day after an order was received. In fact,

ACME had increased its business and he had to hire another person to help him. The computer couldn't pack the boxes.

Since the order records contained the salesperson's code, commissions were automatically credited. The system displayed any outstanding orders, so phone orders could be checked to avoid duplication. The fact that the salespeople were entering their own orders meant that the office staff didn't have to enter them and this cut down on the transaction volume in the office.

The reports on aged receivables permitted Prudence to call potentially delinquent accounts after 30 days and to get many of them to begin payments. The system also prevented additional orders from being taken for customers who were delinquent or over their credit limits.

The reorder limits worked like a charm. Prudence was able to take over the purchasing of the inventory. Mr. Emerson cut his finance costs 50 percent because he had current information about when and what was needed.

He was often discovered after hours seated at the keyboard doing his projections. He developed many ways to look at his numbers, and every time the next idea occurred to him, he couldn't wait to get at the computer to try it out.

Martin Anderson called after the system had been in for a while to see how things were going. Prudence answered the phone. She was very pleased, as was everyone else at ACME. She said she didn't understand how they had managed at all without a computer. "As a matter of fact, we didn't manage very well without one, did we?" she exclaimed.

"Oh, you'll never guess what showed up after the system was up and running. It seems that most of the double-order problem was traced to Mark's customers. There was a discrepancy of almost $5000 worth of watches that had been shipped, not paid for, and not returned. When we contacted the customers, they said Mark had picked up the double orders saying that he would take care of returning them. Since the customers weren't billed twice, they thought that was the end of the matter. Because we were so confused with the inventory and the paperwork, we never caught the problem. Mark had evidently discovered this weakness in our process. Anyway, Mr. Emerson was pretty upset. He threatened to have Mark arrested. Mark paid back the money, and Mr. Emerson let him go. Mark actually had the nerve to ask for a reference. Can you imagine that?"

"What a story," said Anderson. Prudence couldn't see the little smile of satisfaction on his face. So his suspicions had been correct after all. "Please tell Mr. Emerson I called. I'm so glad you are enjoying your system."

Glossary

Access time: The time required to obtain data from main memory or a storage device, such as a diskette or a Winchester disk.

Accumulator: A working register.

ACIA: See Asynchronous Communications Interface Adapter.

Adder: A combinational logic circuit that adds binary numbers.

Address: A binary number that identifies a single location in memory.

Address bus: A bus over which the CPU sends an address to select an individual location in memory.

Algorithm: A series of logical steps to be followed sequentially in order to perform a task or solve a problem.

Alphanumeric: Characters containing both letters of the alphabet and numbers.

ALU: See Arithmetic and Logic Unit.

Analog computer: A computer that uses variable voltages to represent numerical quantities. A specific analog computer is often designed to solve a relatively small number of problems. A computer used most frequently in scientific applications.

Application programs: Programs that perform functions to produce data for end users.

American Standard Code for Information Interchange (ASCII):   A 7-bit code that represents standard bit configurations for 128 alphanumeric characters and several nonprinting characters used to control printers and communication devices.

AND function: A logic function where the output is 1 only if all inputs are 1.

AND gate: A logic gate for the AND function.

Arithmetic and Logic Unit (ALU):   That part of a CPU that performs arithmetic and logical operations in a digital computer.

Assembler: A computer program that translates an assembly language program into a machine language program.

Assembly language: The next step above machine language. Substitutes mnemonics such as LDA or CLR for binary instructions such as 01100111.

ASCII: See American Standard Code for Information Interchange.

ASCII keyboard: A keyboard that sends an ASCII character to a computer when a typist presses the corresponding key.

Asynchronous: A communications method in which data is sent as soon as the computer is ready to send it, as opposed to methods in which data is sent a fixed intervals.

Asynchronous Communications Interface Adapter (ACIA):   A chip that provides a serial connection between the CPU and peripherals.

Background: Refers to one or more noninteractive programs or tasks running on a computer while the user is using another interactive (foreground) task.

Backup: Copying of one or more files onto a storage medium for safekeeping in case the original should be damaged or lost.

BASIC (Beginners' All-Purpose Symbolic Instruction Code):   A widely used interactive programming language developed by Dartmouth College that is especially well suited to personal computers and beginning users.

Base: A number used as the reference for constructing a number system. The decimal system is a base 10 number system.

Batch processing: The technique of running a set of computer programs without human interaction or direction.

Baud: A unit of data transmission speed roughly equal to a single bit per second. Common baud rates are 110; 300; 1200; 2400; 4800; and 9600.

Bidirectional: (1) Ability to transfer data in either direction, especially on a bus. (2) Ability of a print head to print from right to left or left to right, which helps to increase print speeds.

Binary: (1) A number system with only two digits—0 and 1—in which each successive symbol represents the next higher decimal power of two. (2) Any system that has only two possible states or levels, such as a switch that is either on or off. This is represented in a computer circuit by the presence of current (equivalent to "1") or the absence of current (equivalent to "0"). All computer programs are executed in binary form.

Bit: Short for binary digit, either a 0 or a 1. It is the smallest unit of data recognized by the computer. All letters, numbers, and symbols handled by the computer are expressed entirely as a combination of bits.

Bit-mapped graphics: A technology that allows control of individual pixels on a display screen to produce graphic elements of superior resolution, permitting accurate reproduction of arcs, circles, sine waves, or other curved images.

Board: Also circuit board. A plastic resin board containing electronic components such as chips and the electronic circuits needed to connect them.

Branch: A computer program instruction that transfers control from one instruction sequence to another somewhere else in the program.

Buffer: A temporary storage area for data, often used to hold data being passed between the computer and peripheral devices or communications lines which operate at different speeds from the computer.

Bus: A group of parallel electrical connections that carry signals between computer components or devices.

Byte: 8 bits, used to represent a character in the computer.

Carriage return: A control character that causes the print head return from the right side of the platen to the left.

Cathode Ray Tube (CRT):   A vacuum tube that generates and guides electrons onto a fluorescent screen to produce such images as characters or graphic displays on video display screens.

Central Processing Unit (CPU):   Electronic components in a computer that control the transfer of data and perform arithmetic and logic calculations.

Character: A single printable letter (A–Z), numeral (0–9), or symbol (% $,) used to represent data. Text symbols also include those that are not visible as characters, such as: space, tab, and carriage return.

Character printer: A printer that prints one character at a time like a typewriter.

Chip: A thin slice of silicon up to a few tenths of an inch square containing an integrated circuit with dozens to thousands of electronic parts on its surface.

Circuit: (1) A system of semiconductors and related electrical elements through which electrical current flows. (2) In data communications, the electrical path providing one-way or two-way communication between two points.

Clock: A circuit that produces a sequence of regularly spaced electrical pulses to synchronize the operation of the various circuits in a digital computer.

COBOL (Common Business-Oriented Language):   A high-level programming language that is well suited to business applications involving complex data records (such as personnel files or customer accounts) and large amounts of printed output.

Compatibility: (1) The ability of an instruction, program, or component to be used on more than one computer. (2) The ability of computers to work with other computers that are not necessarily similar in design or capabilities.

Combinational logic: A collection of logic gates that responds to incoming information almost immediately and without regard to earlier events.

Compiler: A computer program that translates a high-level computer language into machine language.

Computer: An electronic device that processes discrete (digital) or approximate (analog) data.

Configuration: The assortment of equipment (disk drives, terminals, printers) in a particular system.

Control bus: A bus that transmits control signals.

Control unit: That part of the CPU that directs the fetching and executing of instructions by providing timing and control signals.

Counter: A string of flip-flops that counts in binary.

Core: The older type of nonvolatile computer memory made of ferrite rings that represent binary data by switching the direction of their magnetic polarity. Most modern computers use integrated circuit memories which are faster than core memory but are volatile.

CP/M (Control Program for Microprocessors):   An operating system used by many microcomputers with Intel or Zilog CPU chips.

CPU: See Central Processing Unit.

CRT: See Cathode Ray Tube.

Cursor: A movable, blinking marker, usually a rectangle or line, on the video screen that marks the point of next character entry or change.

Daisywheel: A print head that forms full characters rather than characters formed of dots. It is shaped like a wheel with petals radiating from the center. A letter, numeral, or symbol is located on the end of each petal.

Data: Facts, numbers, letters, and symbols stored in the computer. Basic elements of information used, created, or otherwise processed by an application program.

Data base: A large collection of organized data that serves as a common source for application programs.

Data processing: Applications in which a computer works primarily with data as opposed to text.

Debug: The process of finding and fixing an error in a computer program or in the actual hardware design of a computer.

Decoder: A combination a circuit that converts binary data into some other number system.

Diagnostics: Programs that check the operation of a device, board, or other component for malfunctions and report their findings to the user.

Digital computer: A computer that uses discrete signals to represent data. It can be programmed to solve a wide variety of problems.

Direct Memory Access (DMA):   A method for transferring data to or from a computer's memory without CPU intervention.

DIP: See Dual In-Line Package.

Disk: A rigid, flat, circular plate with a magnetic coating on which bits are stored by means of electromagnetic signals from the disk drive head.

Disk/diskette drive: A unit which causes the disk or diskette to spin and which has a head used for reading from and writing to the disk or diskette surface.

Diskette: A flexible, flat, plastic circle housed in a cardboard envelope and covered with a magnetic coating that stores bits.

Display: A device that shows a visual representation of characters and shapes; a TV-like screen. See Cathode Ray Tube.

Distributed data processing: A computing approach in which an organization uses computers in more than one location, rather than using one large computer in a single location.

DMA: See Direct Memory Access.

Dot-matrix printer: A printer that forms characters from a set of wires whereby each wire produces a dot. The arrangement of the dots creates the various characters, symbols, and graphic pictures.

Double density: A recording method for diskettes that stores twice as many bits as single-density recording on diskettes of the same diameter.

Downtime: The period of time when a device is not functioning and has not yet been fixed.

Drive: See disk/diskette drive.

Dual In-Line Package: A plastic rectangle housing an IC chip and having a row of metal pins protruding from each of its long sides.

Electronic mail: A communications feature that permits short messages to be sent to other terminals or computers.

Emulator: A program that allows a computer to imitate a different program or system, thus enabling different systems to use common data and programs.

Encoder: A combinational circuit that converts data from some other number system into binary.

Ergonomics: The science of human engineering that combines the study of human-body mechanics and physical limitations with industrial psychology.

EPROM (Erasable Programmable Read-Only Memory):   A type of Read-Only Memory that can be erased by applying ultraviolet light and then reprogrammed.

Fanfold paper: Continuous sheets of paper whose pages are folded accordion-style and may be separated by tearing at the page perforations. Used for long documents and internal reports in place of single sheets of paper.

Field: A logical entity upon which a program can act, for example, last name, or weekly pay.

File: A collection of logically related records.

First generation: Digital computers that used vacuum tubes for switching and storing bits.

Flip-flop: The basic sequential logic circuit. A circuit that is always in one of two possible states.

Floppy disk: See diskette.

Flowchart: A diagram that shows the major steps or operations that take place in a computer program.

Font: A set of letters, numerals and symbols of the same type style. Daisywheels are available in different fonts.

Foreground processing: Top-priority processing; it has priority over background processing.

Formfeed: A control character that causes the printer to advance the paper to the top of the next page.

FORTRAN (Formula Translation):   A widely used high-level programming language well suited to problems that can be expressed in terms of algebraic formulas. It is generally used in scientific applications.

Function key: A key on a keyboard that is programmed by means of either hardware or software to cause the computer to perform a specific function, such as clearing the screen.

Garbage: Data that has no meaning in the present context.

Gate: The simplest electronic logic circuit. Composed of one or more transistors.

Gigabyte: 2^{30} or 1,073,741,824 bytes.

Graphics: The use of lines and shapes to display images and data, as opposed to the use of characters.

Hard-copy: Output in permanent form, usually printed, rather than displayed in temporary form such as on a CRT.

Hard disk: A disk that is not flexible. More expensive than floppy diskettes, but capable of storing more bits.

Hardware: The physical components of a computer system.

Hardwired: Refers to a permanent, physical connection between two points in an electrical circuit.

Head: A component that reads and writes on a storage medium such as magnetic disk or tape.

Hexadecimal: A number system with a base of 16.

IC: See Integrated Circuit.

IEEE: Institute of Electrical and Electronics Engineers.

Impact printer: A printer that forms characters on paper by striking an inked ribbon with a character-forming element.

Input: Data entered into a computer to be acted upon by the CPU.

Input/Output (I/O):   The links between the CPU and the outside world.

Input/output port: The location where data enters and leaves a device.

Instruction: A statement that tells the CPU what to do. Consists of an operation plus one or more operands.

Instruction set: A set of operations (op codes) designed for and implemented on a computer.

Integrated Circuit (IC):   A complete electrical circuit composed of many transistors on a single chip.

Interactive: A dialogue, usually carried on through a keyboard and a CRT, between the computer and the user.

Interface: An electronic assembly that connects an external device, such as a printer, to a computer.

Interpreter: A computer program that translates and then executes a computer program a step at a time.

Interrupt: A temporary suspension of program execution so that the CPU can deal with a higher priority task.

Inverter (NOT gate):   A logic gate with one input and one output. The output always has the opposite state from the input.

I/O: See Input/Output.

Job: A task or program.

K: 2^{10} or the decimal value 1024.

Keyboard: The set of keys on a terminal that allows alphanumeric characters and symbols to be transmitted to the computer when the keys are depressed.

Kilobyte (Kbyte or KB):   1024 bytes.

Large-Scale Integration (LSI):   The combining of up to about 10,000 circuits or gates on a single chip.

LED: See Light-Emitting Diode.

Letter quality printer: A printer used to produce typewriter quality documents.

Light-Emitting Diode (LED):   A small device (diode) that produces a red light when turned on.

Linefeed: A control character that causes the printer to advance one line.

Lineprinter: A high-speed printer that prints an entire line of characters at a time. Usually attached to large, mainframe computers.

Logic state: A condition that is either on or off, true or false, and so on. The two logical states are represented by the binary digits 0 and 1 in digital computers.

Loop: A sequence of computer instructions which is repeated one or more times until a desired end condition is achieved.

LSI: See Large-Scale Integration.

Machine language: Binary code which can be executed by a computer.

Macroinstruction: A computer instruction composed of a sequence of microinstructions.

Magnetic tape: Tape reels or cassettes used as mass storage media. A sequential medium used primarily for file backup.

Mainframe: A computer with very powerful hardware and software used for large business and/or scientific applications.

Mask: (1) A bit pattern that shields certain bits in a group from being tested or used. (2) In chip production, a layer that protects certain parts of the chip surface from exposure to impregnation or metalization.

Megabyte (Mbyte or MB): 2^{20} or 1,048,576 bytes.

Memory: A high-speed storage area in a computer for the temporary placement of program instructions and data which the computer is working on.

Memory-mapped I/O: The assignment of specific addresses in memory for input and output to designated peripheral devices.

Microcomputer: A physically small computer containing a microprocessor chip or chips to be used for program execution.

Microinstruction: The most basic operation that a digital computer can execute.

Microprocessor: A single-chip central processing unit manufactured with LSI technology.

Microsecond: One millionth of a second.

Millisecond: One thousandth of a second.

Minicomputer: A computer of size and capabilities between a mainframe and a microcomputer.

Mnemonic: An abbreviation or other set of letters which acts as a memory aid. Assembler language commands are mnemonics.

MOS (Metal-Oxide Semiconductor):   The most common form of semiconductor using LSI technology.

Multiplexer: (1) A combinational circuit that applies the logic state of one of several inputs to a single output. (2) A communication device that combines the signals from several slow-speed lines for transmission over a faster line.

Multiprocessing: Execution of two or more computer programs by a computer that contains more than one central processor.

Multiprogramming: A scheduling technique that allows one CPU to execute more than one program or task at a time by giving each one small slices of time. The computer appears to be multiprocessing, but, in fact, the CPU is only doing one thing at a time. This technique allows printing by one task while another is waiting for input from a keyboard, for example.

Multitasking: See multiprogramming.

Nanosecond: One billionth of a second.

Network: A group of terminals and/or computers that are connected to each other by communications lines.

Nibble: Half a byte, 4 bits.

Nonvolatile memory: Memory that does not lose its contents when power is turned off. Examples are core memory and magnetic bubble memory.

NOT gate: See Inverter.

Object code: Program statements that have been converted to machine (binary) language.

On-line: Connected to and under the control of the CPU.

Operand: The quantity that is operated on, the object of the instruction.

Operation code (op code): A binary or hexadecimal number that serves as a code for a particular operation or instruction.

Operating system: A collection of programs that controls the overall operation of a computer and performs such tasks as managing memory, processing interrupts, scheduling tasks, and controlling input and output to the system.

OR function: A logic function where the output is 1 if one of the inputs is one.

OR gate: A logic gate for the OR function.

Output: Signals or data sent out of the computer by the CPU.

Parallel transmission: Sending several bits over parallel wires simultaneously.

Parity: An extra bit in a character code used to detect memory, I/O, or transmission errors. The total number of bits in the unit of data is totaled and the extra bit is set depending on the parity scheme. If odd parity is used, the total number of bits set including the parity bit must be odd; if even parity is used, the total must be an even number.

Peripheral: A device that is external to the CPU and main memory, for example, printer, modem, terminal, but connected to it electrically.

Pixels (Picture Elements): Locations on a display screen that are addressed individually by the computer and used to form graphic images. Screens with more pixels generally provide higher resolution and sharper images.

Port: A physical area for the connection of a peripheral or communication line to the CPU.

Power supply: A unit in the computer that converts ac power to dc power; energizes components such as integrated circuits, monitors, and keyboards; and steps down the power coming into the computer for certain components that require less power.

Printer: The device that produces a paper copy of a document (hard-copy output).

Printout: Anything printed by a printer; hard copy.

Processor: See Central Processing Unit.

Program: The instructions and routines containing the logic needed to solve a problem or to cause the computer to work.

Programmable Read-Only Memory (PROM):   A type of Read-Only Memory that may be changed by using special equipment.

Programming language: The words, mnemonics, and symbols along with the rules for using them from which computer programs are written. Examples are BASIC, COBOL, and PASCAL.

PROM: See Programmable Read-Only Memory.

RAM (Random Access Memory):   Memory that can be read and written (altered) during program execution. Used to store program instructions and data temporarily for use by the CPU.

Record: A group of related fields or data elements, for example, a customer record.

Register: A string of flip-flops that stores one word of binary data; a temporary memory used by the CPU.

Remote: Not wired directly to the computer; communicating via telephone lines or some other transmission method, for example, microwave, satellite.

Reverse video: A feature on a display unit that produces the opposite combination of colors for characters and background, for example, white characters on a black background where black on white is the normal mode.

ROM (Read-Only Memory):   Memory containing fixed data or instructions that are permanently loaded into it during the manufacturing process and are not changed during the execution of programs.

Second generation: Computers made from discrete transistors rather than integrated circuits.

Semiconductor: A material midway between a metal and an insulator in its ability to conduct electricity, for example, silicon; acts as a switch in response to control signals.

Sequential access: Starting at the beginning and passing through each successive record to get to the one desired. Magnetic tape is a sequential access medium.

Sequential logic: A collection of logic gates that responds to incoming information when a clock pulse is received. Sequential logic circuits use flip-flops which store a logic state (0 or 1) as one input for the next operation.

Serial transmission: Sending one bit after the other over a line.

Single density: A recording standard for the number of bytes to be stored on the surface of a diskette.

Single sided: A diskette on which data is stored on only one side.

Single thread: A simple operating system that executes a single task from beginning to end without interruption before it starts another one. The opposite of a multitasking operating system.

Software: The programs or logic that cause the computer to perform functions.

Solid state: Electronic components that do not have moving parts; made from materials such as silicon and germanium.

Source program: A program written in nonbinary form in a computer language such as BASIC or assembly language.

Synchronous: Taking the same amount of time to transmit each piece of data with no time lapses in between.

Task: A program under execution.

Teletypewriter: A typewriterlike device that can be used to input data into a computer by means of its keyboard and to print output by means of its printer mechanism.

Terminal: An input/output device used to enter data into a computer or to record output from one. Typically refers to a keyboard and CRT or printer.

Third generation: Computers made from integrated circuits.

Timesharing: Providing service to many users by letting each user's task share the resources of a central computer. Users are usually connected to the computer via communication links.

Tractorfeed: An attachment on a printer that has sprockets to fit the holes on the sides of fanfold paper; used to move the paper through the printer.

Transistor: A solid-state device that can be used as an on-off switch.

Turnkey system: A complete system of hardware and software to meet the needs of a particular application. No modifications or changes are needed.

Two-state: Capable of being in one of two states; binary.

VLSI (Very Large-Scale Integration):   The combining of up to 100,000 gates on a single chip.

Volatile memory: Memory that loses its contents when the power is turned off. Usually semiconductor memory.

Winchester disk: A hard disk permanently sealed in a drive unit to prevent contaminants from affecting the read/write head; capable of storing larger amounts of data than a diskette in the same surface area.

Word: The largest number of bits the CPU can handle in one operation. Usually 1 or more bytes.

Word processing: The handling of text by performing such functions as inserting and deleting, rearranging lines and paragraphs, paging, and formatting.

Word wrapping: The automatic shifting of words to the next line when the right margin is reached.

APPENDICES

Binary Arithmetic

A. BINARY ADDITION

The binary number system has two digits, 0 and 1. These are the numbers we use to perform binary addition. The rules for binary addition are as follows:

1. $0 + 0 = 0$
2. $0 + 1 = 1$
3. $1 + 0 = 1$
4. $1 + 1 = 0$ (with a carry of 1, or $1 + 1 + 10$)

A simple table to illustrate the binary addition rules is:

	0	1
0	0	1
1	1	10

Some samples of binary addition are as follows:

```
 1001      1010
  110      1100
 ----     -----
 1111     10110
```

We have a problem when we want to add $1 + 1$ with a previous carry of 1. For example:

```
  101
  111
 ----
 1100
```

Moving from right to left, the leftmost column requires that we add $1 + 1 + 1$. This is the same as adding $1 + 1 = 10$ and then $10 + 1 = 11$. This is sometimes written as $1 + 1 + 1 = 11$, and is called the *fifth* rule of binary addition.

B. BINARY SUBTRACTION

Most computers perform binary subtraction by *adding*. One of the common schemes is by using *two's complement notation*. The complement of a binary number is obtained by inverting the number so that all 0s become 1s and all 1s become 0s. For example, the complement of 1001 is 0110.

To subtract one binary number from another, the number to be subtracted is first inverted. The two numbers are then added and a 1 is added to the result. Any carry is discarded. For example,

1011	1011	
-0011	$+\ 1100$	Inverted number
	10111	Discard the carry
	0111	
	$+\ \ \ \ 1$	
Result	1000	

Our original example: 1011 − 0011 is equivalent to decimal 11 − 3. The result, 1000, is equivalent to decimal 8.

Decimal Equivalents of Powers of 2

2^0	1	
2^1	2	
2^2	4	
2^3	8	
2^4	16	
2^5	32	
2^6	64	
2^7	128	
2^8	256	
2^9	512	
2^{10}	1024	(1K) 1 Kilobyte
2^{11}	2048	(2K)
2^{12}	4096	(4K)
2^{13}	8192	(8K)
2^{14}	16,384	(16K)
2^{15}	32,768	(32K)
2^{16}	65,536	(64K)
2^{17}	131,072	(128K)
2^{18}	262,144	(256K)
2^{19}	524,288	(512K)
2^{20}	1,048,576	(1M) 1 Megabyte
2^{21}	2,097,152	(2M)
2^{22}	4,194,304	(4M)
2^{23}	8,388,608	(8M)
2^{24}	16,777,216	(16M)
2^{25}	33,554,432	(32M)
2^{26}	67,108,864	(64M)
2^{27}	134,217,728	(128M)
2^{28}	268,435,456	(256M)
2^{29}	536,870,912	(512M)
2^{30}	1,073,741,824	(1G) 1 Gigabyte

Binary, Decimal, and Hexadecimal Equivalents

Binary	Decimal	Hexadecimal
0	0	0
1	1	1
10	2	2
11	3	3
100	4	4
101	5	5
110	6	6
111	7	7
1000	8	8
1001	9	9
1010	10	A
1011	11	B
1100	12	C
1101	13	D
1110	14	E
1111	15	F
1 0000	16	10

Index